Vegetarian Flavors
with *Alamelu*

Also by Alamelu Vairavan

Art of South Indian Cooking

Healthy South Indian Cooking

Healthy South Indian Cooking-Expanded Edition

Chettinad Kitchen

Indian Inspired Gluten-Free Cooking

Healthful Indian Flavors with Alamelu

Vegetarian Flavors with *Alamelu*

Wholesome, Indian Inspired, Plant-Based Recipes

Alamelu Vairavan

Photography by Linda Smallpage

Hippocrene Books, Inc.
New York

Foreword by Margaret Pfeiffer, MS, RD

Interior design by K & P Publishing/Barbara Keane-Pigeon.

For further information, contact:
HIPPOCRENE BOOKS, INC.
171 Madison Avenue
New York, NY 10016
www.hippocrenebooks.com

Cataloging-in-Publication Data is available from the Library of Congress.

ISBN 978-0-7818-1412-6

Printed in the United States of America.

CONTENTS

Foreword by Margaret Pfeiffer, MS, RD   1

Introduction by Alamelu Vairavan   2

Shopping List for Spices & Other Basics   4

The Indian Spice Box   6

Multilingual Glossary of Spices &
    Lentils (Dals)   7

Spice and Other Basics in Indian Cooking   8

General Cooking Tips   15

RECIPE CHAPTERS

Appetizers   17

Chutneys, Sauces & Soups   29

Breakfast   47

Rice Dishes   61

Sambhars & Kulambus   91

Vegetable Dishes   115

Desserts   229

Index   235

Acknowledgments   243

About the Author   245

Foreword

I have had the pleasure of knowing Alamelu since 2000. She offered a cooking demonstration with fresh vegetables at ProHealth Waukesha Memorial Hospital in Wisconsin, where I worked as a registered dietitian with cardiac rehabilitation patients. All too often I had heard the complaint that vegetables were tasteless and boring. When Alamelu made her green beans recipe, people were surprised at how much flavor the dish had, and even those who did not like green beans were eating and enjoying them. But even more important to them was how easy the recipe was. Soon they were sharing this recipe with other patients at their exercise class and also bringing this dish to our annual picnic.

The word "vegetarian" suggests some degree of limitation when it comes to eating foods. You do not need to be a vegetarian to enjoy the recipes in this book. There is no single perfect diet for everyone. Each individual will have a unique eating plan that works best for them. However, the one thing that is common to the healthiest eating plans—whether Mediterranean, DASH, Flexitarian, or Modified Keto—is consuming more vegetables by being plant-based. If you are moving vegetables from the side of the plate to the center, the recipes within this book fit those goals. The nutritionally-rich spices that are commonly used in Indian cooking, such as turmeric (curcumin), black pepper, and cumin, are an extra bonus that adds flavor and numerous health benefits. This creates a winning combination of health with taste.

Lentils and vegetables provide the fiber you need for your digestive health. Protein requirements are easily met with a vegetarian diet that consists of a variety of plant-based foods and lentils. Anyone who wants to explore new flavors--healthy people as well as those seeking health—will find Alamelu's book to be a valuable guide. If you have health concerns, this book can be of great help to you too. Scientific research has linked spices and plant-based diets to the prevention of multiple ailments including diabetes, cardiovascular disease, Alzheimers, and even some cancers.

Alamelu has unique culinary expertise and I have had the pleasure to eat some of the tastiest and healthiest dishes prepared by her. If you have seen her on television, attended one of her cooking classes, or have one of her previous cookbooks, you will be familiar with her easy to prepare tasty recipes. If this is your first time learning from Alamelu, you can trust her to lead you through the wonderful world of Indian-inspired vegetarian recipes and will be thrilled with the exciting flavors. Alamelu should be commended for her continued efforts to bring together another collection of recipes for all of us to enjoy.

Margaret Pfeiffer, MS, RD
Registered Dietitian

Introduction

I have a passion for helping people discover and enjoy healthful cooking, especially vegetarian cooking. Through my cooking classes and presentations in wellness programs, food and wine festivals, fund-raising events, schools, libraries, and in hospital community education programs, I have been impressed by people's eagerness to learn vegetarian cooking. Many participants in these events followed up with visits to Indian grocery stores to shop for spices and tried new recipes. The positive responses over many years have been overwhelming.

My previous cookbooks and PBS Create TV shows have featured many vegetarian dishes. Given the growing interest, it was natural for me to consider writing a book exclusively devoted to vegetarian cooking. It was at this time, about three years ago, my editor Priti Gress at Hippocrene Books, New York, also approached me with the idea of a new book that would include a selection of the best vegetarian recipes from my previous books and many new recipes in one volume. In the meantime, I attended vegan and vegetarian food festivals in Naperville, Illinois, and in Scottsdale, Arizona. The events were an eye-opening experience for me. I sensed a deep interest in vegetarian and vegan cooking among thousands of people, and I was inspired to contribute to this expanding culinary world.

In December 2019, when I was still thinking about the possibility of a vegetarian book project, my husband and I flew on a Southwest flight from Dallas to Phoenix. As we rushed onto the plane, barely making the flight on time, I was greeted by the friendly voice of a flight attendant, Jonathan, who was dressed like an elf to reflect the holiday spirit. He said, "Welcome Alamelu, it is a pleasure to have you fly with us today." When I was wondering how he knew me, he told me how much he enjoyed my TV cooking shows on PBS Create that he had seen in Dallas! He added, "I hope you will continue to be the light you are and help people like me to eat better." What a surprise—it was like an affirmation to start my cookbook project!

Inspired by my experience on the flight, and with the encouragement of my husband, I informed my editor of my decision to start my cookbook project. With the COVID-19 pandemic constraining our social life, travel, and other activities, I found it was a perfect time for me to focus on this new cookbook.

The recipes presented in this book use fresh, vibrant vegetables enhanced with spices and lentils that are readily available. They are mostly inspired by South Indian cooking traditions, and are easily adapted to any kitchen. Cooking with plant-based ingredients is deep rooted in India for centuries. It is common for people in South India to switch to vegetarian diets as they get older for health and religious reasons. As the great health benefits of vegetarian foods are becoming better known, more and more people in the West are also leaning towards vegetarian diets. In this book, I present more than one hundred vegetarian recipes, many of which have been selected, sometimes in revised form, from my earlier books. I also present numerous new recipes that I developed for this book. Some of the new recipes feature vegetables like parsnips, kale, and kohlrabi that are not found in South Indian cuisine. These are innovations. In most of the recipes, I added notes for variations and substitutions for some ingredients. Another useful feature of the book is a section on general cooking tips that I would recommend to any beginner before trying the recipes. I have included additional sections on spices and lentils (dals), a shopping list, and suggestions for storing spices.

It is worthy of mention, that once you buy and store the basic spices and lentils, they retain their freshness for months. So it is only vegetables that you need to shop for every week. Another important note is that vegetable and rice dishes cooked with spices and lentils can be stored in the freezer for future use. Spices help retain the quality of cooked food for a long period of time.

In my presentations, people frequently ask what kind of cookware I use in my kitchen. In general, I use good stainless-steel pots and pans, non-stick cookware, sharp knives, a large cutting board, a blender, a spice grinder, and a rice cooker.

As we know all too well, many parents find it a challenge to get their children to eat vegetables. Simply boiled and steamed vegetables are not appealing to children. Through my experience with children, especially in elementary school presentations, I have observed kids eagerly wanting to eat vegetables when the dishes are tasty and cooked with mild seasonings. I believe these recipes will appeal to adults and children alike and will awaken young palates.

Whether you are a beginner or someone who is experienced and eager to try new recipes, this book will be a useful guide in discovering the joy of cooking tasty, plant-based foods. You will be amazed at how quick and easy these recipes are. You will also be surprised to note how a single vegetable can be cooked in many different ways, each dish bringing out different flavors!

I hope your cooking experience will bring you good health and happiness!

Cooking is love,
Alamelu Vairavan
Milwaukee, Wisconsin

SHOPPING LIST FOR SPICES AND OTHER BASICS

Spices:

- ☐ Asafoetida
- ☐ Bay leaves
- ☐ Black mustard seeds
- ☐ Black pepper (whole/ground)
- ☐ Cayenne pepper powder
- ☐ Cinnamon sticks
- ☐ Cumin (seeds/ground)
- ☐ Fennel seeds
- ☐ Fenugreek seeds
- ☐ Red chili pepper (dried whole)
- ☐ Saffron
- ☐ Tamarind paste
- ☐ Turmeric (ground)
- ☐ Cinnamon Sticks
- ☐ Cumin Seeds
- ☐ Fennel Seeds
- ☐ Fenugreek Seeds

Spices Powders:

- ☐ Curry powder (Deep brand)
- ☐ Black pepper and ground cumin powder
- ☐ Chutney powder (MTR brand)
- ☐ Garam masala
- ☐ Sambhar powder (MTR brand)

Nuts:

- ☐ Almonds
- ☐ Cashews
- ☐ Peanuts
- ☐ Coconut, unsweetened shredded (dried or frozen)

Dals (Lentils):

- ☐ Black Gram Dal, split (Urad dal)
- ☐ Yellow lentils (Moong dal)
- ☐ Red lentils (Masoor dal)
- ☐ Yellow split peas (Channa dal)
- ☐ Yellow split pigeon peas (Toor dal)

Short Shopping List to Get Started

- ☐ Black Mustard Seeds
- ☐ Urad dal
- ☐ Cumin Seeds
- ☐ Ground Cumin
- ☐ Ground Turmeric
- ☐ Cayenne Pepper powder
- ☐ Yellow lentils (Moong dal)
- ☐ Red lentils (Masoor dal)

Tips for Buying Spices and Spice Powders

With very few exceptions, the spices used in Indian vegetarian cooking can be found in most regular supermarkets. Other spices can be bought economically from Indian grocery stores (found in most major cities or metropolitan areas in the U.S., Canada, and U.K.) or from stores specializing in spices. One may also order spices on the Internet from many Indian grocery stores or Web sites in the United States, Canada, and UK, including:

http://www.ishopindian.com

http://www.singals.ca

www.amazon.com

The Indian Spice Box

In an Indian spice box there are seven small containers that often hold the following spices:

Black mustard seeds   Fenugreek seeds
Urad dal   Cinnamon sticks
Fennel seeds   Dried red chili pepper
Cumin seeds

Storing Spices and Dals: Most spices and lentils keep best in sealed glass bottles or containers. Tightly closed, spices will retain their quality for many months, and even for a year or two. I highly recommend removing spices, powders, and lentils from their plastic bags as bought from the store and storing them in bottles with identifying labels. Spices kept in the kitchen cupboard in jars will provide easy access to cooking. Stored this way, they will also retain their flavor, aroma, and color. There are various size jars available in spice shops and in discount stores.

Multilingual Glossary of Spices and Lentils (Dals)

This glossary will be helpful in shopping for spices and lentils from Indian grocery stores. Spices are commonly labeled in Hindi (national language of India) in Indian groceries. The Tamil term is also provided, as Tamil is one of the major languages of South India, where I come from.

English	Hindi	Tamil
Asafoetida	Hing	Perungayam
Bay leaf	Tez Patta	Lavangilia
Black Pepper	Kalimirch	Milagu
Cardamom	Elachai	Elakkai
Cinnamon	Dal Chini	Pattai
Chili Peppers	Mirch	Milagaai
Cumin Seeds	Jeera	Jeerakum
Fennel Seeds	Saunf (Sonf)	Perumjeerakum
Fenugreek Seeds	Methi	Venthayam
Mustard Seeds	Rai	Kadugu
Saffron	Zaffron	Kungumappu
Tamarind	Imli	Puli
Turmeric	Haldi	Manjal
Almonds	Badam	Badam
Black Gram Dal (split)	Urad dal	Uluntham Paruppu
Red Gram Dal	Toor dal	Thuvaram Paruppu
Red Lentils	Masoor dal	Mysore Paruppu
Wheat flour	Atta	Gothambai Mavu
Yellow Chickpeas	Chana dal	Kadalai Paruppu
Yellow Lentils	Moong dal	Paasipayaru

Spices and Other Basics in Indian Cooking

SPICES AND SPICE BLENDS

Asafoetida: A strongly scented resin used in small quantities in some vegetable and rice dishes, it imparts a flavor reminiscent of onion and garlic. Asafoetida is sold in lump or powdered form. The powdered form is available in Indian grocery stores.

Bay Leaves: Long, dried green leaves that add a subtle flavor to any dish. Bay leaves have a sweet woody aroma, much like that of cinnamon, and a slightly pungent flavor. They are added to warm oil to enhance the flavor of rice and vegetable dishes and can be removed from a dish before serving.

Black Mustard Seeds: Small, round, black raw mustard seeds have almost no aroma. But on cooking they impart an earthy, nutty aroma. When mustard seeds are dropped in a small amount of hot oil, they pop and crackle as they give out a distinctive flavor. Black mustard seeds are available in spice stores and in Indian grocery stores.

Black Peppercorns: Black pepper is known as the "king of spices." Pepper was valued as much as gold in the thirteenth century. Today pepper is readily available around the world and is used in almost every cuisine as it adds great flavor to many dishes. The taste of black pepper is spicy hot and its aroma is pungent. It is known as an appetite stimulant and as a digestive spice.

Black Pepper and Cumin Powder: Grinding equal parts of whole black peppercorns and cumin seeds together into a fine powder makes an aromatic spice blend (no need to roast before grinding). Alternately, you can mix in equal proportion already ground black pepper and ground cumin sold separately in grocery and spice stores. This spice blend is also a great salt substitute! Delicious when used over fried eggs and in flavored rice and vegetable dishes. Store in a glass jar for use as needed.

Cardamom: Cardamom is a pod consisting of an outer shell with little flavor and tiny inner seeds with intense flavor. Ground cardamom has an intensely strong flavor and is easy to use. Cardamom is known as the "queen of spices." Ground cardamom is used in some rice dishes, desserts, and spiced chai tea.

Cayenne Pepper Powder (Red Pepper Powder): Cayenne pepper powder has the power to make any dish spicy hot, but it also has a subtle flavor-enhancing quality. Cayenne pepper powder mixed with ground cumin adds an amazing flavor to dishes. Usually used in small amounts, the heat of a dish can be controlled by the amount of cayenne pepper powder used.

Chutney Powder: An aromatic blend of spices including coriander seeds, red chili peppers, curry leaves, asafoetida, and toor dal, chutney powder comes prepackaged. I recommend the "MTR brand" that is available in Indian grocery stores and also at amazon.com.

Cinnamon Sticks: The aromatic, reddish-brown bark of the cinnamon tree imparts a rich, sweet flavor to foods. Cinnamon sticks are sometimes cracked down to small slivers to be used in cooking. The taste is warm, sharply sweet, and aromatic. Cinnamon and bay leaf cooked together enhance the flavor of vegetable and rice dishes. Cinnamon sticks can be removed before serving. Ground cinnamon can also be used in place of cinnamon sticks. Add ground cinnamon when adding other ground spices to the dish being prepared.

Cumin Seeds: Cumin seeds are enjoyed for both their aroma and medicinal qualities. The small, oblong, brown seeds resemble caraway seeds and have a peppery flavor. When cumin seeds are dry-roasted or added to warm oil, they impart a rich aroma that enhances rice and vegetable dishes.

Ground Cumin (Cumin Powder): Ground cumin blends well with many spices. Ground cumin blended with cayenne pepper powder or with ground black pepper lends distinctive flavor to any dish (see Black pepper and cumin powder above). Ground cumin is an essential ingredient in curry powder and garam masala powder.

Curry Powder: A blend of many spices such as coriander, fenugreek, cumin, black pepper, red chili pepper, and turmeric, commercial blends of curry powder are readily available in regular grocery and spice stores.

Fennel Seeds: Fennel seeds are a much-used spice in India. Vibrant green, the seeds have a warm, sweet, and intense licorice flavor that turns mild on roasting.

Fenugreek Seeds: Small, hard, oblong brown seeds, fenugreek seeds are slightly bitter in taste but roasting them subdues the flavor. They are an important ingredient in curry powder and saucy dishes.

Urad dal
Black mustard seeds
Cumin seeds

Garam Masala: The heart of most North Indian dishes, garam masala is a blending of several dry-roasted and ground spices, such as coriander seeds, cumin seeds, cardamom, black peppercorns, cloves, cinnamon, and bay leaves. "*Masala*" refers to a combination of several spices and "*garam*" means spice intensity referring to spice richness. Thie spice blend is readily available in most grocery stores.

Sambhar Powder: An aromatic blend of spices and dals including red chili peppers, cumin seeds, curry leaves, fenugreek seeds, asafoetida, chana dal, and toor dal. Sambhar powder is readily available packaged as "Madras Sambhar Powder" (MTR brand) in Indian grocery stores and also at amazon.com.

Turmeric (Ground/Powder): One of the great Indian spices and known as Indian gold, ground turmeric is a yellow root that has been dried and powdered. It imparts a musty flavor and bright yellow color to any dish. Turmeric contains the compound curcumin and is recognized by many as an antioxidant, anti-cancer, and anti- inflammatory substance. Growing research suggests that turmeric may help prevent arthritis and a host of other diseases including Alzheimer's. Lately turmeric has been the subject of study by many scientists and physicians who are embracing the natural benefits it provides.

RICE AND GRAINS

Rice: Rice is a comfort food throughout the world. Four types of rice, commonly used in our recipes for rice dishes, are outlined here.

Basmati Rice: A fragrant, high-quality rice used in making both plain and flavored rice dishes, basmati rice has a nutlike flavor and comes packaged under several brand names. When purchasing basmati rice, look for a quality brand such as Dehradun or Tilda. They are available in natural food stores and Indian grocery stores. The grains of basmati rice are finer than the grains of other types of rice, and they separate beautifully after they are cooked. Basmati rice is unexcelled in making flavored rice dishes.

Brown Rice: Although white and basmati rice are commonly used in South Indian cooking, you may also prepare the recipes in this book with brown rice. You may find that the nutty flavor and high fiber content of the brown rice compensates for its lack of lightness and delicacy.

Rice and quinoa

Extra-Long-Grain Rice: This rice is used in making plain and flavored rice dishes. It lacks the aromatic quality of the basmati and jasmine rice, but it is a good all-purpose rice. It is available in regular supermarkets.

Jasmine Rice: This is a delicate and aromatic pure white rice. It is excellent for making plain or flavored rice dishes. It is available in Indian grocery stores as well as many regular supermarkets.

Quinoa (*pronounced keen-wa*): A hardy and nutritious grain with a unique texture and taste, quinoa is a gluten-free complete protein source. Qunioa comes in many colors including tan, red,orange, pink, purple and black.

Cooking Rice and Quinoa: To cook any type of rice, I highly recommend an automatic electric rice cooker. Rice cookers are readily available in department stores and on the Internet. Rice cookers come in various sizes, ranging from a small, four-cup size to larger sizes.

DALS

Dals (Lentils): Legumes are high in protein and fiber, and are a staple ingredient in many South Indian dishes. There are numerous varieties of dals, but in most recipes no more than two varieties of dals are needed. The most common of these are toor dal (or toovar dal) and urad dal. The following is a broad array of dals:

Masoor Dal (Red Lentils): An orange-red colored lentil, also known as red lentil, masoor dal in split form is used in making *sambhars*. Masoor dal cooks faster than toor dal and can be substituted for toor dal in *sambhars* and other vegetable dishes. Masoor dal is available in natural food stores and Indian grocery stores.

Moong Dal (Yellow Lentils): A golden yellow lentil used in split form, this most versatile of dals cooks quickly and is widely used in making vegetarian dishes. The whole moong bean, which is small, oval, and olive green in color, is called whole green gram dal. Available in Indian grocery stores.

Toor Dal / Toovar Dal: A kind of yellow lentil that is split into two round halves, toor dals sometimes are packaged in a slightly oiled form. Toor dal is cooked to a creamy consistency to make sambhars, kootus, and soups. It creates the rich base so characteristic of delicious sambhars. Toor dal is available in Indian grocery stores.

Urad Dal: A creamy white split lentil. Fried urad dal gives a nutty, crunchy taste to dishes. Essential to South Indian cooking, urad dal is used both as a seasoning and as a base for *dosais*. Urad dal, fried in oil with black mustard seeds and various other seasonings, is an essential ingredient in many recipes. Available in Indian grocery stores. (Note: Urad dal, when whole, has a black skin and is known as black gram lentil. The recipes in this book use the split urad dal exclusively.)

Yellow Split Peas: A familiar kind of legume, readily available in regular grocery stores. Yellow split peas appear often in the recipes in this book because of their distinctive texture and taste. Specifically yellow split peas are used to make dishes such as *vadas* (vegetable fritters) and stir-fried vegetables. (Very similar to yellow split peas is chana dal, available in Indian grocery store.)

 Cooking dals: Dals are very easy to cook. In each recipe where dals are used, I have given easy-to-follow stovetop cooking instructions. Pressure cookers are often used in Indian households to cook toor dal as it takes more time to cook this type of dal.

Yellow split peas
Masoor dal /Red lentils
Moong dal /Yellow lentils

COOKING OILS

Two types of light vegetable oils are preferred in preparing Indian flavored dishes—**canola oil** for its mild flavor and **corn oil** for its rich corn taste. You may also use extra-virgin olive oil or coconut oil, but the taste of the dishes will be slightly different. For Vegans I suggest almond butter or coconut oil.

Ghee: Also called clarified butter, ghee is used in preparing delicious rice and dessert dishes. Ghee is made by melting butter, then straining off the solids. You can discard the solid residue or it is often used for making delicious ghee rice. Store ghee, covered, at room temperature or in the refrigerator. When you wish to use ghee, heat a small portion in a butter warmer and use as needed. Ghee adds a wonderful flavor to dishes, but should be used sparingly because of its high-fat content.

OTHER INGREDIENTS

Cilantro (Coriander Leaves): A distinctively aromatic herb, the fresh cilantro leaves are of major importance in Indian cuisine. Cilantro is also used both as a garnish and for making chutneys. The dried seeds of the cilantro plant, called **coriander seeds**, are also use in Indian cuisine either whole or ground.

Coconut: The edible inner flesh of the coconut is widely used as a garnish for cooked vegetables and as a base for chutneys and sauces. Shredded fresh coconut in frozen form is available in the freezer section of Indian, Mexican and Thai grocery stores. At home, after purchase, unwrap the packet and keep coconut in a bowl for a few minutes to thaw. Then using your fingers, break the frozen coconut into shreds in the bowl. Store this thawed, shredded coconut in sandwich bags (with about one cup of coconut in each bag) for future use. Keep in freezer and use as needed. Unsweetened shredded dry coconut powder is available in Indian and natural food stores. Store dry shredded coconut in a bottle in the spice cabinet. It can be used as a substitute for fresh shredded coconut.

Shredded coconut and curry leaves

Curry leaves: Leaves from the tropical curry leaf trees, fresh curry leaves lend a uniquely appealing aroma to Indian cooking. It is not uncommon to find curry leaf trees grown in South Indian homes. Curry leaves are distinct from curry powder. When sautéed in oil, curry leaves enrich the flavor of vegetarian dishes including chutneys, stir-fries, saucy dishes, flavored rice dishes, and buttermilk drinks. Indian grocery stores stock fresh curry leaves year round. The leaves with tender stems are packed in small plastic bags, and are inexpensive, usually about a dollar a bag. Fresh curry leaves when refrigerated can stay fresh for a week.

Garlic: This bulbous herb composed of individual cloves is an essential ingredient in South Indian cooking and is used in most sauces and vegetable dishes to enhance flavor. When sautéed in hot oil, garlic infuses the entire dish with a distinctively pleasing flavor. Garlic and ginger make a delicious combination in enhancing many vegetable dishes.

Ginger Root: A root spice with a warm, fresh flavor that is used often in Indian cooking, both as a basic ingredient and as a garnish. Fresh ginger is highly recommended for its flavor and healthful qualities. Ginger can be shredded and stored in a bottle in the refrigerator for long term use. Besides being using in preparing vegetable dishes, shredded ginger can also be used to make chai.

Green Chili Peppers (Serrano, Jalapeno, Thai Chilies): Fresh unripe chili peppers are a common ingredient that impart a spicy, hot flavor to many Indian dishes. There are a wide variety of chili peppers and you may use any of the many types available, depending on the amount of heat you prefer. Chilies may be used sparingly, however, or omitted altogether depending on your taste. In general, the smaller the chili pepper, the hotter it is.

Mint: A fragrant herb with a uniquely fresh flavor and aroma, mint is used in Indian cuisine primarily in cooling chutneys and relishes that balance the spicier dishes.

Onions: A staple ingredient valued for its flavor and medicinal qualities, onions sautéed in oil with various spices are the foundation of most savory Indian dishes. Onions are also used in yogurt salad and as a garnish for other dishes. Red onions can be used as a colorful garnish for many dishes.

Tamarind Paste: These brown pod-like fruits from the tamarind tree when ground to a paste impart a uniquely sweet and sour taste. This paste adds tartness to dishes. Tamarind is known as the "Indian Date." Bottled tamarind paste is available in Indian grocery stores. Since the bottled paste is very thick, dilute the needed amount of paste with one to two teaspoons of water before using it in a recipe. If tamarind paste is not available, use lemon juice as a substitute.

Tomato sauce: In this book, I have listed the use of regular canned tomato sauce that is readily available in American grocery stores. I usually choose a no-salt-added tomato sauce, as this gives a better flavor with less sodium. Use of tomato sauce facilitates in preparing thick sauces in reduced time. (Note: You can also use fresh, plump ripe tomatoes placed in a blender and pureed into a sauce in place of the canned tomato sauce.)

Whole Dried Red Chili Peppers: Chilies have a strong, sharp aroma and their taste ranges from mild to hot. The level of heat is dependent on the amount of "capsaicin" present in the seeds. Red chili peppers are available fresh, dried, powdered, flaked in oil, and in sauce form, bottled, or pickled. When a whole dried red chili pepper is added to hot oil the flavor of the infused oil gives a very rich, full-bodied taste to dishes. You may remove the whole pepper before serving.

A Word about Using Spices and Chilies

Spices have intrinsic health benefits. There is growing evidence that because of their antioxidant and anti-inflammatory properties spices like turmeric have a healing power in treating or preventing many diseases. Spices also add flavor to foods, reducing a need for salt.

Some people may be reluctant to try recipes with spices fearing that they do not enjoy hot and spicy foods. But rest assured that the recipes in this book do not have to be too spicy or hot. The hotness of a dish comes mostly from chilies or cayenne pepper powder. You can use chilies and cayenne in small quantities (as presented in the recipes here) in such a way that they do not overwhelm the vegetables, but add subtle flavors and aromas to the dishes. Vegetable and rice dishes come alive when enhanced by spices and herbs. The result can be tasty and aromatic foods that are hard to resist. You can transform even broccoli, Brussels sprouts, spinach, cabbage, and lima beans into dishes that are tasty and visually appealing. You may be amazed how even vegetable haters can be transformed into vegetable lovers when spices and legumes are used in cooking.

Besides giving foods a "kick", chilies have nutritional values. For instance, ounce for ounce, green chili peppers have twice as much vitamin C as an orange and contain more vitamin C than a carrot. Chili peppers increase circulation and can warm you up on a cold day. Studies have shown that chili peppers do not aggravate, and may even help those with ulcers and gastrointestinal problems. Eating chili peppers is a good way to curb appetite and control cravings. The compound "capsaicin" found in chili peppers is anti-inflammatory and has antioxidant properties.

General Cooking Tips

1 Relax and enjoy cooking. Preparing the dishes presented in this book does not require a precise measurement of the ingredients. If you add a little more or less than the amount specified in the recipe, you are not going to spoil the preparation.

2 If you don't have a specific spice or other ingredient listed in the recipe, don't be disheartened. Instead of mustard seeds and urad dal, for example, you may use whole cumin seeds. In a very short time, you will become familiar with the spices and possible substitutions.

3 Use plump, ripened, round tomatoes. By adding more tomatoes, you can cut down on the tomato sauce if you prefer. In some recipes, however, tomato sauce enhances the flavor of the vegetable dish and adds richness to the sauce.

4 Most cities have Indian grocery stores. It is also possible to order spices online (see section on "shopping list" for website suggestions).

5 Any leftovers can be refrigerated or frozen with no detriment to flavor or nutritional value. Place leftovers in a plastic microwave dish or in a glass container. Most leftovers can be refrigerated for 3 to 5 days or kept frozen for several months. Just reheat and enjoy.

6 Recipes are easy to follow. I recommend assembling all your ingredients first. Once you have done this, it usually takes less than 30 minutes to prepare a dish. The more practiced you become in preparing a recipe, the easier it will become.

7 A word about vegetables: Even if you don't like a certain vegetable, you may be surprised at how much its taste is transformed and enhanced when prepared with spices and lentils using recipes from this book. I have found that brussels sprouts and lima beans, for example, have won new fans when seasoned with spices. Allow this book to expand your taste and that of your family to include a variety of nutritious vegetables in your daily diet.

8 Storing vegetables in reusable and washable produce cotton mesh bags in a refrigerator will keep the vegetables fresh for more than a week. These bags are available on amazon.com.

9 You can make an entire dinner early in the day and leave dishes at room temperature until dinnertime. Advance preparation actually enhances the flavor of the dishes. Before serving, heat and enjoy.

10 Regular stainless steel heavy-bottomed saucepans, nonstick pots and pans, and woks can be used in cooking the recipes in this book. An electric rice cooker, blender, spice grinder, and stainless-steel steamer are essential.

11 Combining Indian and western dishes makes for a very interesting and pleasing dining experience. Indian rice and vegetable dishes can be inviting additions to a western meal that your family and friends will enjoy.

12 Spices are inexpensive, readily available and have a long shelf life. They do not have to be purchased weekly. They can be purchased as needed. (For storage of spices see page 6.)

Appetizers

Black Bean Cutlets

[Makes 10 cutlets]

 These easy, tasty vegetable cutlets can do double duty as an appetizer or flavorful veggie burgers. With or without a bun, they are delicious served with any chutney!

1 (15-ounce) can black beans drained and rinsed (divided)

¼ cup sour cream or suitable non-dairy option

2 tablespoons fresh lemon juice

¼ teaspoon ground cumin

¼ teaspoon salt more or less to taste

¼ teaspoon ground black pepper

1 teaspoon garam masala

¼ teaspoon cayenne pepper powder more or less to taste

½ medium onion chopped

2 teaspoons oil

½ cup finely chopped green, red, or yellow bell pepper

½ cup chopped fresh cilantro

½ cup breadcrumbs

1 Put half of the beans in a bowl and reserve. Place the remaining beans in a food processor and add the sour cream (or non-dairy option), lemon juice, cumin, salt, pepper, garam masala, and cayenne pepper powder and process until smooth.

2 Spoon the bean mixture into the bowl with the reserved beans.

3 Sauté onion in oil on medium heat until translucent. Add bell pepper and cook 1 minute longer while stirring.

4 Add cooked onion and peppers to the bowl with the bean mixture. Add cilantro and breadcrumbs. Stir to blend evenly.

5 Using ¼-cup portions, form the mixture into round patties. Brush or spray the patties with oil and brown on both sides in pan. Serve with chutney.

Potato Cutlets

[Makes 14 cutlets]

 Delicious seasoned mashed potatoes are used to prepare these crispy golden brown cutlets.

2 medium Idaho potatoes with skins cut in quarters

½ teaspoon ground turmeric divided

1 teaspoon salt divided

2 tablespoons oil

2 to 4 curry leaves optional

½ teaspoon black mustard seeds

½ teaspoon urad dal

1 cup chopped onions

½ cup chopped tomatoes

1 fresh green chili pepper chopped

1 tablespoon minced fresh ginger

½ teaspoon cayenne pepper powder

¼ cup minced fresh cilantro leaves

1 Use the ingredients to prepare Potato Masala as instructed on page 195 and then let the mixture cool.

2 Preheat oven to 400°F.

3 Using 1 tablespoon of potato mixture for each cutlet, form into balls and flatten into round cutlets. Spray cutlets with cooking spray or brush with oil.

4 Place the cutlets on a baking sheet. Bake on each side for 3 to 5 minutes. (If desired, cook in a skillet: place potato cutlets in a lightly-oiled, heated skillet and brown the cutlets on both sides until golden brown.)

Roasted Vegetable Kebabs

[Makes 8 kebabs]

 Roasting brings out the slightly sweet flavors of vegetables. Combined with aromatic spices, they make a tasty, nutritious appetizer or side dish.

8 metal or wooden skewers (if using wooden skewers, soak them in water for 30 minutes)

1 tablespoon oil

½ teaspoon ground cumin

1 teaspoon curry powder

½ teaspoon smoked paprika or **⅛ teaspoon cayenne pepper powder** more or less to taste

¼ teaspoon salt more or less to taste

2½ cups vegetables cut into pieces, such as:

> **½ medium zucchini** cut in half lengthwise, then in half circles

> **½ medium yellow squash** cut in half lengthwise, then in half circles

> **1 cup red, green, and/or yellow bell pepper cubes**

> **½ cup baby portabella mushrooms** cut in half

1 Preheat oven to 425°F.

2 In a plastic resealable bag combine oil, cumin, curry powder, smoked paprika (or cayenne), and salt. Add vegetables, seal, and turn bag several times until spices and oil are evenly distributed.

3 Thread vegetables onto skewers alternating varieties.

4 Place kebabs in a single layer on a heavy-duty rimmed baking sheet. (Dark baking sheets work best to brown vegetables; do not use a light-colored pan or aluminum foil as they prevent vegetables from browning quickly.)

5 Place in oven and roast about 7 minutes. Check to see if they are starting to brown. If not, return to the oven for 3 to 5 more minutes.

6 Turn and bake about 7 minutes longer or until vegetables are cooked as you like them. The time will vary based on your individual oven and the vegetables used.

Lentil Fritters (Masala Vadai)

[Serves 4]

 Vadais are delicious South Indian savories. These fried lentil fritters can be served as appetizers, as a snack at tea time, or as an accompaniment to any meal.

1 cup yellow or green split peas (chana dal)

2 whole dried red chili peppers

1 teaspoon cumin seeds

1 teaspoon fennel seeds

1 garlic clove peeled and chopped

1 cup chopped onions

¼ teaspoon ground turmeric

½ cup chopped fresh cilantro

2 tablespoons grated ginger

1 teaspoon salt

1 cup plain dried breadcrumbs

Oil for frying

1 Soak split peas in approximately 2 cups of warm water for about 3 hours.

2 Drain and grind split peas with red chili peppers, cumin seeds, fennel seeds, and garlic with just enough water in a blender to form a coarse mixture (similar to corn meal). (Note: It is best to grind about ½ cup of soaked split peas mixture at a time with only enough water (approximately ¼ cup) added each time to facilitate the grinding process. Do not grind the split peas mixture too finely. It is desirable to have it coarsely ground to lend a crunchy texture to the finished vadais.)

3 Remove split pea mixture from blender and place in a large bowl. Use your hand to blend the ground mixture thoroughly. Add onions, turmeric, cilantro, ginger, and salt to the mixture. Blend thoroughly by hand.

4 Add breadcrumbs to the mixture and combine until it reaches a consistency sufficiently thick to form a ball. More breadcrumbs may be added if the mixture is too watery.

5 Heat enough oil in a wok for deep-frying. Oil should not be too hot nor smoking.

6 Take a small portion of the ground mixture (about 1 heaping tablespoon) in the palm of your hand and form a ball. With fingers, flatten ball into the shape of a patty. The patty should be about 2 inches in diameter.

7 Drop one or two patties at a time into the heated oil and fry until golden brown on both sides. Remove vadais from hot oil with a perforated spatula and drain them on a plate lined with paper towels. Continue until all patties are fried.

VARIATIONS

Beet Fritters (Beet Vadais): add ¼ **cup finely shredded, peeled fresh beets** along with other ingredients in step 4.

Spinach Fritters (Spinach Vadais): add **1 cup finely chopped baby spinach** along with other ingredients in step 4.

Savory Rice Lentil Balls (Kolakkatai)

[Makes about 20 balls]

 A popular South Indian savory! These ground rice and lentil balls enhanced with coconut can be enjoyed as an appetizer or as a snack with any chutney.

1 cup extra long-grain rice
1 teaspoon cumin seeds
¼ cup yellow lentils (moong dal)
2 tablespoons oil
2 to 4 curry leaves (optional)
1 teaspoon black mustard seeds
1 teaspoon urad dal
1 teaspoon salt
¼ cup fresh ground coconut or
    unsweetened shredded coconut

1 Soak rice and cumin seeds in 3 cups of water for about an hour.

2 Soak moong dal separately in half a cup of water for an hour.

3 Drain water from the rice completely. In a blender grind rice and cumin seeds with ¼ cup of water to a coarse mixture. Transfer to a bowl.

4 Drain moong dal completely. Mix the drained dal with ground rice mixture. Set aside.

5 Heat oil in a non-stick skillet over medium heat. When oil is hot, but not smoking, add curry leaves, mustard seeds, and urad dal. Stir until mustard seeds pop and urad dal turns golden about 20 seconds.

6 Add the ground rice and moong dal mixture to the skillet. Add salt and about 1½ cups of water. Cook, covered over medium heat until ground mixture is cooked, about 15 minutes, stirring often.

7 Add coconut and mix well. Transfer mixture to a bowl. When the mixture is warm to touch, take about a tablespoon of the mixture and make it into an oval shaped ball. Repeat with remaining mixture.

Chutneys, Sauces & Soups

Eggplant Chutney

[Makes 2 cups]

 This is a simple, quick version of traditional eggplant chutney that is still packed with authentic flavor!

2 tablespoons oil

1 whole dried red chili pepper more, if desired

2 cups unpeeled chopped eggplant

½ cup coarsely chopped onions

½ cup coarsely chopped tomatoes

2 garlic cloves peeled and cut in half

½ teaspoon ground turmeric

2 thin slices fresh ginger

½ cup tomato sauce

½ teaspoon salt more, if desired

½ cup warm water

½ teaspoon tamarind paste diluted with 1 teaspoon water; or ½ teaspoon fresh lemon juice

1 Place oil in a warmed skillet. When oil is hot, add red chili pepper, eggplant, onions, tomatoes, and garlic. Stir-fry for about 2 minutes.

2 Add turmeric, ginger, and tomato sauce. Stir well. Add salt. Cover and cook over medium heat until eggplant becomes soft, about 5 to 7 minutes.

3 Transfer mixture from skillet to a blender or food processor and grind. Add warm water and grind to a thick paste.

4 Transfer eggplant mixture to a serving bowl and stir in tamarind paste or lemon juice. Mix well. Serve or refrigerate until ready to serve.

Cilantro Chutney

[Makes 1 cup]

This vibrant green chutney is a popular item in Indian cuisine. My version is creamy with the addition of buttermilk or plain yogurt. If you're looking for a non-dairy option, you can use coconut cream. Cilantro chutney is relatively easy to prepare and packed with flavor. Serve it alongside most appetizers as a dip or with breakfast items such as Dosais (page 52) or Uppumas (page 51).

3 cups chopped fresh cilantro

1 fresh green chili pepper or red pepper

¼ cup chopped onions

¼ cup unsweetened shredded coconut

1 tablespoon grated fresh ginger

6 plain cashews

1 teaspoon lemon juice

½ teaspoon salt

½ cup plain yogurt or coconut cream

½ cup warm water

Place all the ingredients in a blender. Grind and process until a smooth, thick consistency and blended well. Transfer to a bowl. Refrigerate until ready to serve. (Chutney can keep in the refrigerator for 2 to 3 days.)

Eggplant in Seasoned Tamarind Sauce (Kosamalli)

[Serves 4]

 This seasoned eggplant sauce is a specialty of the Chettinad region of South India. The eggplant is cooked to perfection with onions and tomatoes in tamarind sauce. This delicious sauce can be enjoyed with Multigrain Savory Crepes (page 49), Dosais (page 52), naan or toasted bread.

3 cups chopped eggplant with skin

1 cup chopped onions

¼ cup chopped tomatoes

1 fresh green chili pepper chopped (more, if desired)

2 tablespoons oil

4 to 6 curry leaves

¼ teaspoon asafoetida powder

1 teaspoon black mustard seeds

1 teaspoon urad dal

¼ teaspoon ground turmeric

½ teaspoon cayenne pepper powder

½ teaspoon ground cumin

1 teaspoon salt

½ teaspoon tamarind paste

½ cup tomato sauce

¼ cup chopped fresh cilantro leaves

1 Put the chopped eggplant in a saucepan with 3 cups of water. Cook, uncovered, for a few minutes until eggplant becomes soft. Mash undrained eggplant and set aside. (You could peel eggplant if you prefer not to use the skin.)

2 Mix onions, tomatoes, and green chili pepper in a small bowl and set aside.

3 Heat oil in a saucepan over medium heat. When oil is hot, but not smoking, add curry leaves, asafoetida powder, mustard seeds, and urad dal. Fry until mustard seeds pop and urad dal turns golden brown, about 30 seconds.

4 Immediately add onion mixture and cook until onions are tender.

5 Add the turmeric and mix well. Add the mashed eggplant and stir to combine. Add cayenne pepper powder, cumin, salt, tamarind paste, and tomato sauce and stir to combine.

6 Add 2 cups of water and stir. When the mixture begins to boil, add the cilantro leaves and let sauce simmer over medium heat for 5 to 7 minutes.

Seasoned Apple Relish

[Makes 1 cup / Serves 4]

 There are so many ways to enjoy this apple relish with a kick. You can, for example, spread it on toast or crackers for a savory-sweet snack. It can also be enjoyed as an accompaniment to Multigrain Savory Crepes (page 49).

2 tablespoons oil

1 teaspoon black mustard seeds

1 Granny Smith apple unpeeled and shredded

½ teaspoon ground turmeric

¼ teaspoon ground cumin

¼ teaspoon cayenne pepper powder more or less to taste

¼ teaspoon salt more or less to taste

1 Heat oil in a skillet over medium-high heat. When the oil is hot but not smoking, add mustard seeds and cook and stir until seeds start to pop.

2 Add apple, turmeric, cumin, cayenne pepper powder, and salt. Cover and cook 2 to 3 minutes.

3 Scrape into a dish and serve warm or cold.

 Variation
To make Creamy Apple Chutney Dip add ½ **to 1 cup yogurt or a non-dairy substitute**. Enjoy as a great dip with fresh vegetables or crackers.

Peanut and Coconut Chutney

[Makes 1½ cups]

 This chutney pairs perfectly with Dosais (page 52) or Multigrain Savory Crepes (page 49) and also works as a spread on sandwiches or as a side with toasted naan bread.

1 cup dry-roasted unsalted peanuts

¼ cup grated fresh coconut or unsweetened dried coconut

3 garlic cloves peeled and cut in half

1 whole dried red chili pepper more or less to taste

¼ teaspoon salt more or less to taste

¾ to 1 cup warm water

1 Place peanuts, coconut, garlic cloves, chili pepper, salt, and ¾ cup warm water in a blender or food processor; blend or process until smooth.

2 If the chutney seems too thick, add additional water, 1 tablespoon at a time. Scrape into a dish and serve.

Tomato and Onion Chutney

[Makes 1 cup]

 This bright, zesty chutney is an excellent staple to keep on hand in the refrigerator. It adds instant flavor as a spread in sandwiches and wraps. This chutney can also be enjoyed with Dosais (page 52) and Multigrain Savory Crepes (page 49).

2 tablespoons oil

1 whole dried red chili pepper more or less to taste

½ teaspoon black mustard seeds

½ teaspoon urad dal

½ cup chopped onions

½ cup chopped tomatoes

¼ teaspoon ground turmeric

¼ teaspoon cayenne pepper powder more or less to taste

¼ teaspoon ground cumin

¼ teaspoon salt more or less to taste

½ cup tomato sauce

1 tablespoon minced fresh cilantro

1 Heat oil in a skillet over medium-high heat. When the oil is hot but not smoking, add chili pepper, mustard seeds, and urad dal and stir a minute or two until mustard seeds start to pop.

2 Add onion and tomatoes to skillet; cook and stir until onions are translucent.

3 Add turmeric, cayenne, cumin, and salt. Stir and cook for a few minutes until mixture is well-blended.

4 Stir in tomato sauce and 2 tablespoons water. Cook for a minute or two. Stir in cilantro. This chutney can be stored in the refrigerator for up to 2 days.

 VARIATION
To make Tomato and Onion Raita cool the above chutney and then stir in **1 cup of whisked plain yogurt or a non-dairy substitute**.

Carrot and Lentil Soup with Kale

[Serves 4 to 6]

 This hearty, fiber-rich vegan soup is a meal unto itself. Lentil soup gets a makeover with aromatic ginger, spices, and kale.

½ **medium onion** chopped

½ **tablespoon oil**

½ **pound (2 to 3 medium) carrots** peeled and chopped

1 **garlic clove** finely chopped

½ **tablespoon grated fresh ginger**

½ **fresh green chili pepper** chopped (more or less to taste / for less "heat" use green bell pepper)

½ **cup masoor dal (red lentils)**

2½ **cups reduced-sodium vegetable broth**

1 **cup low-sodium spicy vegetable juice** or **1 cup water with about ¼ teaspoon cayenne pepper powder added**

½ **teaspoon ground turmeric**

½ **teaspoon ground cumin**

1 **cup chopped kale leaves** stems discarded

1 **tablespoon minced fresh cilantro**

1 In a 4-quart stockpot over medium heat, sauté the onion in the oil until softened.

2 Add carrots, garlic, ginger, chili pepper, and masoor dal, and sauté for a few minutes.

3 Add broth, vegetable juice (or water and cayenne), turmeric, and cumin. Bring to a boil, then reduce to a simmer, cover, and cook for 15 to 20 minutes or until carrots are as soft as you like them.

4 Add kale and cook 3 more minutes.

5 If soup is too thick, add up to 2 cups of hot water till desired thickness. Simmer on low-medium heat for 3 minutes. Serve garnished with cilantro.

Cauliflower Lentil Soup

[Serves 4 to 6]

 Lentils add protein and fiber to this aromatic dal-based soup that features cauliflower and tomatoes. The flavors of cinnamon and cardamom give this soup a lovely depth. It makes for a warm, filling, and comforting lunch or dinner.

¼ cup masoor dal (red lentils) or **moong dal (yellow lentils)**

½ teaspoon ground turmeric divided

2 tablespoons oil

3 (½-inch-long) slivers cinnamon stick

1 bay leaf

½ medium onion sliced lengthwise

1 cup chopped tomatoes

½ fresh green chili pepper minced (more or less to taste)

¾ cup tomato sauce

4 cups hot water

¼ teaspoon ground cardamom optional

2 teaspoons ground cumin

½ teaspoon salt more or less to taste

2 cups (1-inch pieces) cauliflower florets

2 tablespoons minced fresh cilantro

VARIATIONS

To make **Beet & Lentil Soup**, you can use about **1 cup thinly sliced beets** in place of the cauliflower.

To make Tomato-Lentil Soup, replace the cauliflower in the above recipe with about ½ **to 1 cup of chopped tomatoes** and skip step 5.

1 Bring 2 cups of water to a boil in a deep saucepan. Add lentils and ¼ teaspoon turmeric. Reduce heat to medium and cook, uncovered, for about 30 minutes, until lentils are soft and creamy. Do not drain. Reserve.

2 Heat oil in a deep saucepan over medium heat. When the oil is hot but not smoking, add cinnamon stick and bay leaf and stir a few seconds.

3 Add onion slices, tomatoes, green chili pepper, and remaining ¼ teaspoon turmeric. Cook and stir, uncovered, until onions and tomatoes are tender.

4 Add tomato sauce and reserved lentils with water. Stir in 4 cups of hot water. Add cardamom, cumin, and salt and stir well. Cook, uncovered, over medium heat until mixture begins to boil.

5 Reduce heat. Add cauliflower and cook, uncovered, about 2 minutes or until cauliflower is just tender. Do not overcook cauliflower.

6 Add cilantro, simmer a few minutes. Remove from heat. Serve immediately or cover and set aside off heat until ready to serve. Briefly reheat before serving.

Sweet Potato Quinoa Soup

[Serves 6]

 Quinoa is not actually a grain, but rather the seeds of a green leafy plant. It is gluten-free and rich in protein. Quinoa, sweet potatoes, corn, and two kinds of beans come together beautifully in this hearty soup.

½ cup quinoa

1 medium onion chopped

2 teaspoons oil

5 cups reduced-sodium vegetable broth

2 teaspoons ground cumin

½ teaspoon ground turmeric

¼ teaspoon cayenne pepper powder more or less to taste

1 cup fresh cut green beans

¼ cup frozen corn

2 cups peeled and cubed sweet potatoes

1 (15-ounce) can reduced-sodium white beans (cannellini, navy, or chickpeas) drained and rinsed

¼ cup chopped fresh cilantro

1 Rinse quinoa in several changes of water and drain in a fine-mesh strainer. Reserve.

2 In a 3-quart saucepan over medium heat, sauté onion in oil about 3 minutes or until onion is translucent. Add reserved quinoa and stir for a few minutes.

3 Add broth, cumin, turmeric, and cayenne. Bring to a boil, then reduce heat, cover, and simmer for 10 minutes.

4 Add green beans, corn, and sweet potatoes. Bring back to a boil, then reduce heat, cover, and simmer for 5 to 10 minutes, until sweet potatoes are tender.

5 Add white beans and cilantro; heat for 2 minutes and serve.

Breakfast

Multigrain Savory Crepes (Adais)

[Makes 15 crepes / Serves 4 to 6]

 These nutricious multigrain, gluten-free lentil crepes are called "adais" in South India. Adai batter does not require fermentation. These crepes are easy to prepare and are typically served with any type of chutney or with Kosamalli (page 35). Adais also make a wonderful sandwich wrap—spread wrap with fillings and chutney, roll up, and enjoy.

½ cup yellow split peas

¼ cup masoor dal (red lentils)

½ cup moong dal (yellow lentils)

½ cup extra-long-grain rice

2 whole dried red chili peppers more or less to taste

1 teaspoon cumin seeds

1 teaspoon fennel seeds

½ teaspoon ground turmeric

½ teaspoon salt more or less to taste

½ cup minced onion

1 tablespoon minced fresh ginger

¼ cup chopped fresh cilantro

1 Soak the yellow split peas, masoor dal, moong dal, rice, red chili peppers, cumin seeds, and fennel seeds in 3 cups of water for 2 hours. Drain and discard water.

2 Place soaked mixture in a blender with 1½ cups of fresh water. Add turmeric, salt, onion, and ginger. Grind to a coarse, thick consistency adding additional water, a tablespoon at a time, if needed. (The batter should be quite thick; you can add more water when making crepes if needed.)

3 Add cilantro and blend a few seconds. The mixture is ready for making the crepes.

4 Heat a skillet over medium heat. Brush with ¼ teaspoon oil or spray with cooking spray. Using ¼ cup of batter for each crepe, spread the batter in the skillet in a circular pattern with the back of a spoon, as thinly as possible. Cook until the crepe becomes crunchy and golden. Loosen the edges with a spatula. Turn over and cook until golden brown, about 1 minute longer. Adjust heat as necessary for even browning. Roll or fold and serve hot.

Cream of Wheat Uppuma

[Serves 4]

 This is a savory, flavorful version of Cream of Wheat cooked with spices. You can serve this uppuma with a sambhar or a chutney. This dish is often enjoyed for breakfast or at afternoon tea.

2 tablespoons oil

1 whole dried red chili pepper

1 teaspoon black mustard seeds

1 teaspoon urad dal

¼ cup finely chopped onions

¼ cup finely chopped tomatoes

1 cup uncooked quick or regular cream of wheat

½ teaspoon salt

1 fresh green chili pepper finely chopped

2 teaspoons minced fresh ginger

2 cups warm water

¼ cup minced fresh cilantro leaves

1 teaspoon unsalted butter

2 tablespoons roasted cashew halves optional

1 Place oil in a skillet over medium heat. When oil is hot, but not smoking, add red chili pepper, mustard seeds, and urad dal and cook for a few seconds until urad dal turns golden.

2 Add onions and tomatoes and cook for 1 minute. Add cream of wheat and stir for 1 minute. Add salt, chili pepper, and ginger. Stir for 1 minute.

3 Gradually add 2 cups of warm water to cream of wheat while stirring. Cover and cook over low heat, stirring frequently, for about 2 minutes.

4 Add cilantro and butter. Stir well. Add cashews, if desired, and mix well.

 VARIATIONS

To make **Vegetable Uppuma**, follow the same recipe but after adding water to cream of wheat, add ¼ cup shredded carrots and ¼ cup frozen (thawed) green peas and stir. Cover and cook over low heat stirring frequently.

To make **Cracked Wheat Uppuma** replace the cream of wheat with cracked wheat; or to make **Quinoa Uppuma** replace the cream of wheat with quinoa.

Dosais

[Makes 16 dosais]

 Thin unsweetened crepe-like pancakes made of rice and urad dal, dosais are delicious at breakfast. They can also be enjoyed at afternoon tea or as a light evening meal. Unique to South India, dosais can be made plain (as in this recipe) or as Onion Dosais or Masala Dosais (see variations). Serve dosais with a chutney or sambhar.

The batter for dosais has to ferment for 6 to 8 hours, so requires planning ahead. Grind the batter a day before you intend to prepare them in order for fermentation to take place. You may make a few dosais at a time. Save the remaining batter in the refrigerator for making dosais at a later time. The batter can be kept for several days in the refrigerator, but do not freeze. The dosai batter is also used to make Uthappams (page 57).

2 cups uncooked extra-long-grain rice	½ cup cooked plain rice
½ cup urad dal	1 teaspoon salt
1 teaspoon fenugreek seeds (optional)	1½ cups warm water

1 Place uncooked rice, urad dal, and fenugreek seeds in warm water to cover. Stir the mixture with your fingers, rubbing it gently to loosen the starches from the grains. Drain and repeat 2 or 3 times until water runs clear. Add enough warm water to cover generously and soak at room temperature for about 3 hours.

2 Drain water and place rice mixture in an electric blender. Add a little warm water to facilitate the grinding process. Grind on high power for several minutes, adding cooked rice a little at a time as it is being ground until you have a fine paste (cooked rice is added to improve the texture of the batter).

3 Pour the creamy fine batter into a deep mixing bowl (be certain that the bowl you are using will allow the batter to double its quantity). Add the salt and mix well with your hand. (It is essential to use your hand for mixing and not a spoon, because the warmth of the hand initiates the fermentation process.)

4 Cover the bowl with a plate and put it in a warm place in the kitchen overnight. (You can also turn just the oven light on and leave the ground batter inside the oven overnight.) Do not use direct heat. The rice batter will begin to ferment and will double in quantity.

5 The next morning the fermented batter will be frothy. Stir the batter with a large spoon for a few minutes and set aside. Now you are ready to make dosais.

6 Place about ¼ cup of batter into the center of a hot 10-inch nonstick skillet. Spread the batter with a spoon by moving it in concentric circles, starting at the inside of the circle and working towards the outside, spreading the batter thinly and evenly.

7 Cover and cook over medium heat for 1 to 2 minutes. To make plain, soft dosai cook only on one side. If added crispiness is desired, when tiny bubbles appear on the dosai in the skillet place about ½ to 1 teaspoon canola oil in the pan around the dosai. Lift the dosai with a spatula and turn over in skillet. After both sides are cooked evenly, transfer the dosai to a serving plate. Repeat with remaining batter. Dosais are often served folded in a semicircular shape.

There are 4 steps to making dosais:
1. Soaking the ingredients for about 3 hours
2. Grinding for less than 15 minutes
3. Fermenting for 6 to 8 hours (overnight)
4. Cooking dosais

Fermenting Note:
Sometimes, because of cold weather, the dosai batter will not ferment. You may place the bowl in a warmed oven to facilitate: just preheat oven to 350 degrees for 10 minutes and then turn off the oven; wait 10 to 15 minutes, then place the bowl with batter, still covered, in the oven.

Sometimes, depending upon the temperature and humidity, you might have the opposite problem and the batter might ferment in a shorter time and may overflow from the mixing bowl. This will still result in good dosais. Discard the overflow (it cleans up easily) and work with the batter in the bowl.

VARIATIONS

To make delicious **Onion Dosais**, sprinkle finely chopped onions on the plain dosais as they are being cooked in Step 7.

To make **Masala Dosais**, first prepare Potato Masala (page 195). Then place 1 to 2 tablespoons of potato masala on one half of the circular dosa just before removing from the skillet. Fold the dosai over the potato masala and pat down with spatula. The dosai should now have a semicircular shape and the masala dosai is ready to be enjoyed!

Wheat-Based Buttermilk Plain Dosais: For an easy, quick, non-traditional way to make dosais use any buttermilk pancake mix that is commercially available. Then, use the following steps: To 1 cup pancake mix add ¾ to 1 cup of water. Batter should not be too thick or too thin. Whisk to a smooth batter. Then follow steps 6 and 7 in the above recipe for plain dosai. (There is no need for fermentation of the batter.

Tofu Scrambler with Asparagus and Carrots

[Serves 4]

 This delightful breakfast dish is not only easy to prepare, but it is also packed with tempting spices and nutritious vegetables.

1 package (14 ounces) organic firm tofu

2 tablespoons oil

1 teaspoon cumin seeds

½ cup chopped onions

½ green chili, chopped (optional)

1 pound asparagus spears cut into pieces (about 2 cups)

½ teaspoon ground turmeric

½ teaspoon salt (more if desired)

1 teaspoon ground cumin

1 cup peeled and shredded carrots

1 Drain the water from firm tofu. Gently wrap tofu with paper towels to absorb excess moisture. Crumble the tofu into a bowl with your fingers and set aside.

2 In a skillet, heat the oil. When the oil is hot, but not smoking, add cumin seeds and stir till brown, about 20 seconds. Add onions and chili and stir for 1 minute.

3 Add asparagus and stir for 1 minute. Add turmeric, salt, and ground cumin.

4 Add crumbled tofu to the skillet and stir for 1 to 2 minutes.

5 Add carrots and stir over low heat for about 1 minute.

Uthappams

[Makes 12 uthappams]

 Uthappams are a pancake-like thick variety of dosais, typically garnished with onions, chilies, cilantro, and carrots. They make a flavorful breakfast treat. Enjoy with sambhar or a chutney!

1 batch Dosais batter (page 52)

6 to 12 teaspoons canola oil

Finely chopped red onion

Finely shredded carrots

Finely chopped fresh green chili peppers
   optional

Finely chopped fresh cilantro

1 Make the batter for Plain Dosais. (Note: this needs to be done the day before.)

2 Heat a nonstick skillet or iron skillet over medium heat. If you are using an iron skillet, spray with nonstick cooking spray.

3 Pour ½ cup of the dosai batter in the middle of the hot skillet and spread it like a small thick pancake about 6 inches in diameter.

4 When tiny bubbles appear on the uthappam in the skillet place ½ to 1 teaspoon oil in the pan around the uthappam. Sprinkle chopped onion, carrots, chili peppers (if using), and cilantro over the uthappam as it cooks. After about 1 minute, turn the uthappam to the other side and cook until the uthappam becomes golden brown.

Pooris

[Makes about 12 / Serves 4]

 Pooris, unleavened Indian wheat breads, are similar to chapatti or roti, except that they are deep-fried. The layers of the bread puff up as they fry and they are always a welcome treat at my table. Pooris can be enjoyed for breakfast, or as a snack or light meal. Serve with Potato Masala (page 195) as a side dish.

1 cup graham wheat flour*
1 teaspoon oil
½ teaspoon salt
¾ cup warm water
Oil for frying

*Pooris can also be made with King Arthur brand 100% wholewheat flour using approximately 1 cup warm water.

1 Place the flour, oil, and salt in a large bowl and mix well with your hand. Add warm water to flour mixture a little at a time and work ingredients with your hands until they form a firm dough without sticking to your fingers.

2 Knead the dough well with lightly oiled hands. Pound dough vigorously into bowl several times. (A food processor may also be used to form the dough.)

3 Roll the dough into a long, cord-like shape using the palms of both hands. Break off small pieces of dough and form into small, smooth balls, approximately the size of a walnut. If large pooris are desired, the dough should be formed into larger equal-size balls.

4 Dab a very small amount of oil on a flat board or work surface. Place a ball of dough on oiled surface and flatten evenly with a wooden rolling pin into a disc approximately 3 inches in diameter.

5 Heat about 2 inches of oil in a small wok. When oil is hot enough (the pooris will puff up only if the oil is hot enough but not smoking), drop one poori into the oil (it is best to fry them one at a time). The poori will sizzle and rise to the surface. Using a slotted spoon, turn the poori over and fry for an additional 10 to 15 seconds until light golden brown.

6 Lift the poori out of the pan with a slotted spoon, drain off the excess oil on paper towels. Repeat with remaning discs. Serve hot.

Rice Dishes

Notes about Rice and Quinoa

RICE

Rice is a universally loved comfort food. The types of rice commonly used in my recipes are basmati, jasmine, and extra long-grain rice. (See page 10 for descriptions of these varieties.)

BASIC COOKING INSTRUCTIONS FOR RICE

In a Rice Cooker:

To cook any type of rice, I highly recommend an electric rice cooker. Rice cookers are readily available from online retailers, in department stores, and Indian and Asian grocery stores. Rice cookers come in various sizes, ranging from a small 4-cup size to larger sizes.

To Cook Rice in a Rice Cooker: Rinse and drain rice 2 to 3 times with warm water to remove starch and other residue, rubbing the rice gently with your fingers to loosen the starches until the water runs clear. Slowly drain the water. Place the rinsed rice and measured amount of water in a rice cooker. For 1 cup of basmati rice or regular rice add 2 cups of warm water. When rice is cooked transfer rice to a bowl.

On the Stove-top:

Rinse 1 cup of rice in warm water 2 to 3 times to remove starch and other residue, rubbing the rice gently with your fingers to loosen the starches. Slowly drain the rice. In a medium saucepan over medium heat, bring 2 cups water to a boil. Add rice. Bring back to a simmer then lower heat and cook, covered, about 15 to 20 minutes, or until rice is tender and water is absorbed. Remove from heat. Let cooked rice sit, covered, 5 minutes. Transfer to a bowl and then fluff the cooked rice before serving.

QUINOA

Hardy, nutritious quinoa makes a great substitute for rice. Interestingly, it is a member of the same food family as spinach, Swiss chard, and beets, and comes in tan, red, orange, pink, purple, and black varieties. Quinoa is gluten-free and contains all nine essential amino acids, making it a complete protein and an excellent nutritional choice. It is also rich in lysine, an amino acid that is only found in low quantities in most grains. Simple, healthy, delicious, and easy to prepare, it is available in regular and natural food stores.

BASIC COOKING INSTRUCTIONS FOR QUINOA:

To rinse quinoa, use a sieve with a fine enough mesh to trap the tiny seeds. Immerse the sieve in a big bowl of cold water until the seeds are all covered with water. Rub the seeds with your fingers to help remove the saponin. Lift the strainer with the seeds out of the water. Change the water in the bowl. Repeat 2 or 3 times until the water is clear and no foam forms on the surface.

Once the quinoa is rinsed, to 1 cup quinoa add 2 cups of water in a saucepan. Bring to a boil and then reduce the heat to simmer and cover. Cook about 15 minutes or until the germ separates from the seed. The cooked germ looks like a tiny curl and should have a slight resistance when you eat it. Remove from heat and allow to sit for 5 minutes. Fluff gently with a fork and serve. (Quinoa can also be cooked in a rice cooker using the same measurements.)

For a nuttier taste, after rinsing try dry roasting the quinoa in a skillet for about 5 minutes before adding the water and cooking.

Bell Pepper and Tomato Rice with Cashews

[Serves 4 to 6]

 This hearty, flavorful, and nutritious rice dish can be served with any meal. It makes a colorful, splendid addition to the table, especially at Thanksgiving or any holiday dinner.

1 cup basmati rice or extra-long-grain rice

1 tablespoon oil

1 tablespoon unsalted butter

2 to 4 (½-inch-long) slivers cinnamon stick

1 bay leaf

½ teaspoon cumin seeds

½ teaspoon fennel seeds

½ cup onion slices cut lengthwise

¼ cup diced tomato

1 cup coarsely chopped green bell peppers*

¼ teaspoon ground turmeric

1 teaspoon curry powder

1 teaspoon salt

¼ cup tomato sauce

¼ cup cashew halves

1 tablespoon chopped red onion

---

*Or use a combination of green, red, and orange bell peppers for a multi-colored pepper rice.

1 Cook rice according to directions on page 63. Transfer rice to a bowl or platter. Allow rice to cool for a few minutes. Fluff gently to separate the grains. Reserve.

2 Heat oil and butter in a skillet or wok over medium heat. When oil is hot, but not smoking, add cinnamon sticks slivers, bay leaf, cumin seeds, and fennel seeds. Brown for a few seconds.

3 Add onion slices and tomato and stir-fry for 1 minute.

4 Add bell peppers, turmeric, curry powder, and salt. Mix well.

5 Stir in tomato sauce. Cook, covered, over medium heat, until bell peppers become slightly tender, approximately 1 minute, stirring occasionally. (Do not over cook the bell peppers.)

6 Add cooked rice to skillet/wok and gently stir well with sauce. Immediately reduce heat and stir in cashew halves and red onions. Fluff and mix the rice. Serve warm.

Black Pepper and Cumin Rice

[Serves 4 to 6]

 This rice showcases the tasty, aromatic combination of ground black pepper and cumin. A distinctly savory rice dish that goes well with vegetables, it's also a great dish to pack for lunches and picnics.

1 cup jasmine, extra-long-grain, or basmati rice

2 tablespoons oil

1 whole dried red chili pepper more or less to taste

½ teaspoon black mustard seeds

½ teaspoon urad dal

1 cup chopped yellow onions

2 teaspoons Black Pepper and Cumin Powder (page 8)

½ teaspoon salt more or less to taste

¼ cup dry roasted cashews or any toasted nut desired

1 tablespoon finely chopped cilantro

1 Cook rice according to directions on page 63. Transfer rice to a bowl or platter. Allow rice to cool for a few minutes. Fluff gently to separate the grains. Reserve.

2 Heat oil in a large skillet over medium-high heat. When the oil is hot, but not smoking, add chili pepper, mustard seeds, and urad dal and stir until mustard seeds start to pop and urad dal turns golden.

3 Add onions and cook for 1 minute while stirring.

4 Add reserved cooked rice, Black Pepper and Cumin Powder, salt, and cashews and stir until blended. Garnish with fresh cilantro. Stir rice gently and serve.

Vibrant Carrot Rice Pilaf

[Serves 4 to 6]

 Cashews add subtle flavor to this bright, colorful carrot rice dish. It pairs well with almost any main dish—a sure winner on the dinner table.

1 cup jasmine, extra-long-grain, or basmati rice

1 tablespoon unsalted butter

1 tablespoon oil

1 bay leaf

1 or 2 (½-inch-long) slivers cinnamon stick

½ teaspoon cumin seeds

½ cup sliced onion cut lengthwise

½ teaspoon ground cumin

1 teaspoon salt

1 cup shredded carrots

½ cup roasted cashew halves

1 tablespoon minced fresh cilantro

Thinly sliced red onion for garnish

1 Cook rice according to directions on page 63. Transfer rice to a bowl or platter. Allow rice to cool for a few minutes. Fluff gently to separate the grains. Reserve.

2 Heat butter and oil over medium heat in a wide saucepan. When butter is hot, but not smoking, add bay leaf and cinnamon stick. Stir-fry for 1 minute. Add cumin seeds and stir-fry for 20 seconds.

3 Add onion slices and cook for 1 minute. Add reserved cooked rice, ground cumin, salt, and carrots. Fluff rice and carrots gently on low heat.

4 Garnish with cashews and sliced red onion.

VARIATION
To make **Carrot and Peas Rice with Cashews** just add ½ **cup thawed frozen peas** when you add the carrots.

Hearty Cauliflower Rice

[Serves 4 to 6]

 This tempting rice dish is cooked with cauliflower and garnished with cashews and red onions. It makes a very satisfying main dish at lunch or dinner.

1 cup jasmine, extra-long-grain, or basmati
    rice

1 tablespoon oil

1 tablespoon unsalted butter

1 bay leaf

2 to 4 (½-inch-long) slivers cinnamon stick

½ teaspoon cumin seeds

1 cup thinly sliced red onions

2 cups cauliflower florets

1 teaspoon Black Pepper and Cumin Powder
    (page 8) or more if desired

1 teaspoon salt

¼ cup roasted cashews

2 tablespoons chopped red onions

1 teaspoon melted butter optional

1 Cook rice according to directions on page 63. Transfer rice to a bowl or platter. Allow rice to cool for a few minutes. Fluff gently to separate the grains. Reserve.

2 Put oil and butter in a wide-bottomed skillet over medium heat. When oil and butter are hot, but not smoking, add bay leaf, cinnamon sticks, and cumin seeds and stir over medium heat until cumin seeds change color, about 10 seconds.

3 Add onions and cauliflower and stir-fry for a few minutes.

4 Add Black Pepper and Cumin Powder and salt. Cover, cook over medium heat until cauliflower is crisp-tender, about 2 minutes.

5 Add cooked basmati rice. Stir well into cauliflower mixture. Cover and allow to steam over low heat until rice becomes softer and absorbs the flavor of the cauliflower. Add cashews and red onion. Fluff the rice gently.

6 Optional step: 1 teaspoon of melted butter may be added to rice mixture before serving to enhance the flavor. Mix gently.

Chickpea and Apple Rice

[Serves 4 to 6]

 This savory rice enhanced with protein-rich chickpeas and green apples makes an irresistible dish. A sure winner at any meal, it is also great for potlucks and picnics.

1 cup jasmine, extra-long-grain, or basmati rice

1 tablespoon oil

1 tablespoon unsalted butter

1 whole dried red chili pepper

½ teaspoon black mustard seeds

½ teaspoon urad dal

1 cup canned chickpeas drained and rinsed (more, if desired)

1 cup peeled and finely chopped Granny Smith apples

2 tablespoons grated fresh ginger

1 teaspoon minced fresh green chili peppers more if desired

1 tablespoon fresh lemon juice

½ teaspoon ground turmeric

½ teaspoon salt more or less to taste

1 Cook rice according to directions on page 63. Transfer rice to a bowl or platter. Allow rice to cool for a few minutes. Fluff gently to separate the grains. Reserve.

2 Heat oil and butter in a skillet over medium-high heat. When the oil is hot but not smoking, add red chili pepper, mustard seeds, and urad dal; stir until mustard seeds start to pop and urad dal is golden.

3 Add cooked rice, chickpeas, apple, ginger, green chili pepper, lemon juice, turmeric, and salt. Mix well and cook over medium-low heat for 1 to 2 minutes.

VARIATION
To make **Chickpea and Mango Rice**, use **1 cup green, unripe, peeled and chopped mangoes** in place of the apples.

Coconut Rice

[Serves 4]

 This seasoned rice with coconut and cashews is an exquisite and festive side dish.

½ cup jasmine, extra-long-grain, or basmati rice

1 cup fresh unsweetened shredded coconut*

2 tablespoons oil

½ teaspoon asafoetida powder

1 whole dried red chili pepper

2 to 4 curry leaves optional

1 teaspoon black mustard seeds

1 teaspoon urad dal

¼ cup roasted cashew halves

1 teaspoon salt

1 tablespoon chopped fresh cilantro

1 teaspoon coconut oil (optional)

---

*Fresh shredded coconut is available in Indian and Mexican grocery stores in the freezer section.

1 Cook rice according to instructions on page 63. Transfer rice to a bowl or platter. Allow rice to cool for a few minutes. Fluff gently to separate the grains. Reserve.

2 Heat a non-stick skillet or wok and dry roast the shredded coconut on low heat, stirring constantly, about 2 minutes. Remove coconut from skillet/wok and set aside (this removes water content from fresh coconut).

3 Heat oil in the skillet or wok over medium heat. When oil is hot, but not smoking, add asafoetida powder, red chili pepper, curry leaves, mustard seeds, and urad dal. Cover and fry until mustard seeds pop and urad dal turns golden brown, about 30 seconds.

4 Add cooked rice and mix well. Stir in the roasted coconut and mix well. Add cashews, salt, and cilantro. Mix well.

5 Optional step: Warm 1 teaspoon coconut oil and add to the rice and gently fluff.

Fragrant Lemon Rice

[Serves 4 to 6]

 Enriched with lemon juice, ginger, and seasonings, this rice smells divine and makes a delicious accompaniment to any meal. It keeps well at room temperature and can also be packed for lunches and picnics.

1 cup jasmine, extra-long-grain, or basmati rice

¼ cup fresh lemon juice

1 teaspoon salt

½ teaspoon ground turmeric

2 tablespoons oil

1 whole dried red chili pepper

½ teaspoon asafoetida powder

2 to 4 curry leaves optional

1 teaspoon black mustard seeds

1 teaspoon urad dal

2 teaspoons chutney powder

½ chopped fresh green chili pepper optional

3 tablespoons grated fresh ginger

½ teaspoon grated lemon peel

¼ cup dry-roasted unsalted peanuts optional

2 tablespoons minced fresh cilantro

1 Cook rice according to instructions on page 63. Transfer rice to a bowl or platter. Allow rice to cool for a few minutes. Fluff gently to separate the grains. Reserve.

2 Combine lemon juice, salt, and turmeric in a small bowl. Set aside.

3 Heat oil in a large skillet or wok over medium heat. When oil is hot, but not smoking, add red chili pepper, asafoetida powder, curry leaves, mustard seeds, and urad dal. Cover and heat until mustard seeds pop and urad dal is golden brown, about 30 seconds.

4 Immediately stir in lemon juice mixture and chutney powder. Simmer 1 minute, reducing heat if mixture starts to boil.

5 Reduce heat to low. Add cooked rice and stir gently.

6 Add green chili pepper, ginger, and lemon peel. Stir and fluff seasoned rice gently. Serve garnished with peanuts (if desired) and cilantro.

Savory Mushroom Rice

[Serves 4 to 6]

 This simply prepared rice dish can be served with vegetarian main courses. It goes especially well with Potato Kurma (page 191) and Vegetable Kurma (page 223).

1 cup jasmine, extra-long-grain, or basmati rice

1 tablespoon unsalted butter

1 tablespoon oil

1 bay leaf

1 teaspoon cumin seeds

½ cup chopped onions

2 cups chopped mushrooms (portabella, cremini, etc.)

1 teaspoon Black Pepper and Cumin Powder (page 8)

½ teaspoon salt

1 Cook rice according to instructions on page 63. Transfer rice to a bowl or platter. Allow rice to cool for a few minutes. Fluff gently to separate the grains. Reserve.

2 Heat butter and oil in a skillet or wok. When oil is hot, but not smoking, add bay leaf and cumin seeds. Heat until cumin seeds are golden brown, about 30 seconds.

3 Add onions and sauté for a few minutes.

4 Add mushrooms and sauté for a few additional minutes over medium heat. Add Black Pepper and Cumin Powder and salt. Stir and mix over low heat.

5 Add cooked rice and blend well.

Spinach Lentil Rice

[Serves 4 to 6]

 What could be better than fluffy basmati rice combined with a richly-seasoned spinach and lentil dish? Comfort food at its finest! This dish is an excellent accompaniment to vegetable side dishes or yogurt salad.

1 cup cooked **Spinach with Lentils and Coconut** (page 121)

1 cup cooked and fluffed rice

½ teaspoon ground cumin

¼ cup unsalted roasted cashews

1 Prepare the Spinach Poriyal with Lentils and Coconut.

2 In a skillet, combine cooked rice with spinach mixture over low to medium heat. Fluff rice gently. Add ½ teaspoon cumin, if desired.

3 Garnish rice with cashews and serve.

Tomato Rice with Green Onions

[Serves 4 to 6]

 This easy-to-prepare fragrant rice is a colorful addition to any meal.

1 cup jasmine, extra-long-grain, or basmati rice

1 tablespoon oil

1 tablespoon unsalted butter

1 dried bay leaf

1 or 2 (½-inch-long) slivers cinnamon stick

½ teaspoon cumin seeds

½ teaspoon fennel seeds

½ cup chopped onions

1 cup chopped tomatoes

¼ teaspoon ground turmeric

1 teaspoon curry powder

¼ cup tomato sauce

½ teaspoon salt

½ cup chopped green onion tops

¼ cup roasted cashews

1 Cook rice according to instructions on page 63. Transfer cooked rice to a bowl and fluff. Set aside to cool for about 10 minutes.

2 Place oil and butter in a wok or wide-bottomed skillet and heat over medium heat. When oil is hot, but not smoking, add bay leaf, cinnamon stick slivers, cumin seeds, and fennel seeds. Fry until cumin seeds are golden, about 30 seconds.

3 Add onions and tomatoes and sauté for a few minutes. Add turmeric, curry powder, and tomato sauce. Stir well and reduce heat to low. Continue cooking uncovered for 1 to 2 minutes.

4 Add salt and mix well. Add cooked rice and fluff into mixture. Add green onions and cashews and stir gently.

Onion Tomato Raita

 This is an excellent accompaniment for Vegetable Biriyani (page 87) and other flavored rice dishes.

1 cup plain yogurt

¼ cup sour cream

1 cup chopped red onions

1 cup chopped tomatoes

½ teaspoon salt

½ teaspoon ground black pepper

¼ cup finely chopped cilantro

Whisk yogurt and sour cream in a bowl. Stir in red onions and tomatoes. Season with salt and black pepper. Garnish with cilantro. Enjoy!

Creamy Yogurt Rice

[Serves 4]

 A cooling and satisfying yogurt rice that is traditionally served as a final course in a South Indian meal. To ensure a creamy consistency for this dish, you might use a potato masher to soften the cooked rice.

1 cup cooked extra-long-grain or jasmine rice*

2 cups plain yogurt

½ cup buttermilk optional

1 teaspoon minced fresh ginger

1 teaspoon grated fresh lemon zest

½ teaspoon salt

1 Put rice, yogurt, and buttermilk in a bowl and mix well. More yogurt may be added, if desired.

2 Add ginger, lemon zest, and salt. Mix well and serve.

Note: You can also prepare Yogurt Rice in advance, refrigerate, and serve cold.

---

*To achieve a creamy consistency when cooking the rice, cook ½ cup rice with 1½ cups of water.

 VARIATION

To make **Savory Yogurt Rice**, after you have mixed the Yogurt Rice, place **1 teaspoon oil** in a small saucepan and heat until hot but not smoking. Add **½ teaspoon black mustard seeds** and **½ teaspoon urad dal** and cook until mustard seeds pop and urad dal is golden, about 30 seconds. Pour the mixture over the yogurt rice and mix well. Garnish with **2 tablespoons chopped fresh cilantro**.

Photo at left:
Creamy Yogurt Rice
Savory Yogurt Rice

Vegetable Biriyani

[Serves 4]

 Biriyani is an aromatic, festive Indian rice dish, cooked with a variety of colorful vegetables in this vegetarian version. This rice dish can be enjoyed with Onion Tomato Raita (page 84), Potato Kurma (page 191), or Mushroom Cashew Kurma (page 181). It is perfect for celebrations or family gatherings.

1 cup basmati rice

1 cup peeled and cubed potato cut ½-inch cubes

2 tablespoons butter divided

1 tablespoon oil

2 or 3 curry leaves optional

1 whole bay leaf

2 to 3 slivers cinnamon stick

½ teaspoon cumin seeds

1 cup sliced onions cut lengthwise

1 tablespoon minced garlic

1 tablespoon shredded ginger

½ teaspoon ground turmeric

1 cup chopped green bell pepper

½ cup 1-inch cauliflower pieces

½ teaspoon curry powder

½ teaspoon garam masala

1 teaspoon salt

1 cup peeled and shredded carrots

1 cup frozen green peas, thawed

¼ cup sliced red onions thinly sliced lengthwise

¼ cup cashew halves

1 Rinse rice thoroughly in cold water and drain. Bring 2 cups of water to a boil in a saucepan and cook rice over medium heat (or cook rice in a rice cooker). Transfer the cooked rice to a bowl and gently fluff. Set aside.

2 Steam or par-boil potatoes till they are tender. Set aside.

3 Heat a wide-bottomed saucepan over medium heat. Add 1 tablespoon butter and the oil. When butter is melted, but not smoking, add curry leaves, bay leaf, cinnamon stick slivers, and cumin seeds. Sauté until bay leaf becomes light brown, about 15 seconds. Immediately add onions, garlic, ginger, and ground turmeric. Cook until onions are translucent, about 1 minute.

4 Add par-boiled potatoes, green bell peppers, cauliflower and 1 tablespoon of water. Stir and cook on low heat for about 2 minutes.

5 Add curry powder, garam masala, and salt. Gently stir and cook for 1 to 2 minutes.

6 Transfer cooked rice to the vegetable mixture and gently stir. Add shredded carrots and green peas and gently stir.

7 Garnish with sliced red onions and cashews. Gently stir. Add remaining 1 tablespoon of butter. Mix well and serve the vegetable biriyani warm.

Colorful Vegetable Quinoa

[Serves 4 to 6]

 This is an easy way to enjoy a flavorful and nutritionally rich vegetarian dish!

1 cup quinoa (may use red or white)
1 tablespoon oil
1 teaspoon cumin seeds
¼ cup finely chopped onions
¼ teaspoon grated fresh ginger
½ cup frozen peas and carrots thawed
2½ cups hot water
¼ teaspoon salt more or less to taste
¼ cup minced fresh cilantro
2 tablespoons chopped toasted cashews

1 To rinse quinoa: using a sieve with a fine enough mesh to trap the tiny seeds, immerse the sieve in a big bowl of cold water until the seeds are all covered with water. Rub the seeds with your fingers to help remove the saponin. Lift the strainer with the seeds out of the water. Change the water in the bowl. Repeat this step 2 or 3 times until the water is clear and no foam forms on the surface. Drain quinoa and reserve.

2 Heat oil in a 2-quart saucepan over medium-high heat. When the oil is hot but not smoking, add cumin seeds and stir until seeds change color from light brown to semi-dark brown.

3 Add onions and ginger and sauté for a few minutes over medium heat. Add the rinsed quinoa and cook for 1 minute while stirring. Add thawed peas and carrots, hot water, and salt; reduce to a simmer. Cover and cook over low heat for about 15 to 20 minutes or until all of the water is absorbed.

4 Fluff quinoa with a fork. Add cilantro and cashews; fluff with fork and serve hot.

Sambhars & Kulambus

WHAT IS SAMBHAR?

Vegetables and dals (lentils) cooked with sambhar powder (a spice blend that is readily available) to make a hearty sauce with a medium-thick consistency. There are a wide variety of sambhars prepared with an array of vegetables. You can serve sambhars over rice or other grains or with breakfast items.

In South India sambhars are traditionally prepared with toor dal. In this book, I recommend using masoor dal or moong dal because they take far less time to cook than toor dal.

WHAT IS KULAMBU?

A thick vegetable sauce usually made without dals (lentils), Kulambu features numerous individual vegetables cooked with tamarind paste and a variety of spices. Kulambu can also be enjoyed with plain rice and toasted breads.

DALS

Dals are very easy to cook. In each recipe where dals are used, I provide easy-to-follow stovetop cooking instructions. Pressure cookers are used often in Indian households to cook all types of legumes.

*See pages 11 for a description of the dals used in the recipes in this book.

Bell Pepper and Radish Sambhar

[Serves 4]

 In this richly flavored vegetable dish, bell peppers and radishes are cooked with spices in a wholesome lentil sauce. This sambhar is delicious served over plain rice or quinoa and as a dipping sauce with Uppuma (page 51), Dosais (page 52), or toasted naan.

½ cup masoor dal (red lentils) or moong dal (yellow lentils)

½ teaspoon ground turmeric divided

2 tablespoons oil

¼ teaspoon asafoetida powder

1 whole dried red chili pepper

½ teaspoon fenugreek seeds

1 teaspoon black mustard seeds

1 teaspoon urad dal

½ cup chopped onions

½ cup coarsely chopped tomatoes

1 cup thinly sliced white or red radishes

½ teaspoon tamarind paste

2 teaspoons sambhar powder

1½ teaspoons salt

1 cup tomato sauce

2 cups coarsely chopped green bell peppers

1 tablespoon chopped fresh cilantro leaves

Note: If the finished sambhar is too thick, add an additional ½ to 1 cup of warm water.

1 Bring 3 cups of water to a boil in a deep saucepan. Add masoor dal or moong dal and ¼ teaspoon turmeric. Reduce heat to medium and cook, uncovered, for about 30 minutes until dal becomes creamy (if water evaporates during the cooking process, add up to another cup of water). Set aside.

2 Put oil in a saucepan over medium heat. When the oil is hot, but not smoking, add asafoetida powder, red chili pepper, fenugreek seeds, mustard seeds, and urad dal. Cook, covered, until mustard seeds pop and other ingredients are golden brown, about 15 seconds.

3 Add the onions and tomatoes and cook for 1 minute. Add the remaining ¼ teaspoon turmeric and radishes. Cook over medium heat, stirring constantly, for 1 minute.

4 Add tamarind paste, sambhar powder, and salt. Stir and then add the creamy dal mixture and 2 cups of warm water. Stir and cook for 5 to 7 minutes.

5 Add tomato sauce. When the mixture begins to boil add green bell peppers. Cover and cook over low heat for 2 to 3 minutes. (Do not overcook the green peppers.) Add fresh cilantro and serve.

Brussels Sprouts Kulambu

[Serves 4]

 The slightly bitter flavor of Brussels sprouts is balanced by sweet and sour tamarind in this vegetable dish. This saucy dish is best served over plain rice or as a side dish.

2 cups fresh Brussels sprouts cut in half
(if large, cut in quarters so all about same
size)

2 tablespoons oil

¼ teaspoon asafoetida powder

2 to 4 curry leaves optional

½ teaspoon fenugreek seeds

½ teaspoon black mustard seeds

½ teaspoon urad dal

½ cup chopped onions

½ cup chopped tomatoes

4 garlic cloves quartered

¼ teaspoon ground turmeric

3 teaspoons sambhar powder

1 cup tomato sauce

¼ teaspoon tamarind paste

1 teaspoon salt

1 Place cut Brussels sprouts in a steamer and steam for about 3 to 4 minutes until crisp tender. Set aside.

2 Place oil in a saucepan over medium heat. When the oil is hot, but not smoking, add asafoetida powder, curry leaves, fenugreek seeds, mustard seeds, and urad dal. Cover and cook over medium heat until the mustard seeds pop and urad dal is golden brown, about 15 seconds.

3 Add onions, tomatoes, garlic, and turmeric. Stir for 1 minute. Add steamed Brussels sprouts and stir with spices to coat.

4 Add sambhar powder, tomato sauce, tamarind paste, and salt. Stir well. Add 2 cups of warm water to saucepan. Stir and cook for about 5 minutes.

5 Cover and cook over low heat until Brussels sprouts are just tender, about 10 minutes. Be careful not to overcook.

Butternut Squash in Tamarind Sauce

[Serves 4]

 Butternut squash, peeled and cut into cubes, is readily available in many grocery stores. Butternut squash cooked with Indian seasonings in tamarind sauce is uniquely different and delicious. This dish can be enjoyed with rice, quinoa, or any bread.

12 ounces (about 2 cups) pre-cut butternut squash (Note: should be cut evenly into small cubes)

3 tablespoons oil

2 to 4 curry leaves optional

¼ teaspoon fenugreek seeds

1 teaspoon black mustard seeds

1 teaspoon urad dal

½ cup chopped onions

½ cup chopped tomatoes

¼ teaspoon ground turmeric

2 teaspoons sambhar powder

1 teaspoon salt

½ teaspoon tamarind paste diluted with ½ cup water

1 cup tomato sauce

2 cups warm water

1 Place the butternut squash in a microwaveable bowl. Add two sprinkles of water over squash and microwave for about 2 minutes and set aside.

2 Heat oil in a saucepan over medium heat. When oil is hot, but not smoking, add curry leaves, fenugreek seeds, mustard seeds, and urad dal. Stir until mustard seeds pop and urad dal turns golden brown, about 30 seconds.

3 Add onions and tomatoes. Stir and cook until onions are tender.

4 Add ground turmeric and blend well. Add butternut squash and stir into seasonings for about 1 minute.

5 Add sambhar powder and salt and stir well for about 1 minute.

6 Add diluted tamarind paste. Stir well. Add tomato sauce and 2 cups of warm water and stir. Cook, covered, over medium heat until squash is just tender, about 7 minutes.

7 Let the sauce simmer on medium heat, partially covered, stirring often until squash is cooked. (If the sauce thickens before squash is soft add ¼ cup of warm water and stir.)

Carrot Sambhar

[Serves 4]

 Carrots cooked with spices in a lentil base, this sambhar is delicious served over plain rice ot quinoa and as a dipping sauce with Uppuma (page 51), Dosais (page 52), or toasted naan.

½ cup masoor dal (red lentils) or moong dal (yellow lentils)

½ teaspoon ground turmeric divided

2 tablespoons oil

1 whole dried red chili pepper

¼ teaspoon asafoetida powder

2 to 4 curry leaves optional

¼ teaspoon fenugreek seeds

½ teaspoon black mustard seeds

½ teaspoon urad dal

½ cup chopped onions

¼ cup chopped tomatoes

1 cup peeled and thinly sliced fresh carrots

2 teaspoons sambhar powder

¼ teaspoon tamarind paste

½ cup tomato sauce

1 teaspoon salt more if desired

1 tablespoon chopped fresh cilantro leaves

1 Bring 3 cups of water to a boil in a deep saucepan. Add masoor dal or moong dal and ¼ teaspoon turmeric. Reduce heat to medium and cook, uncovered, for about 20 minutes until dal becomes creamy (if water evaporates during the cooking process, add up to another cup). Set aside.

2 Place oil in a large saucepan over medium heat. When oil is hot, but not smoking, add whole red chili pepper, asafoetida powder, curry leaves, fenugreek seeds, mustard seeds, and urad dal. Cook, covered, until mustard seeds pop and other ingredients are golden brown, about 15 seconds.

3 Add onions, tomatoes, and remaining ¼ teaspoon turmeric and stir-fry for 1 to 2 minutes. Add carrots and stir-fry for 1 minute.

4 Add sambhar powder, tamarind paste, tomato sauce, and salt. Cook, covered, over medium-low heat for 3 minutes, stirring occasionally.

5 Add cooked dal and 2 cups of warm water, and stir. Add cilantro. Cook, covered, over medium-low heat for another 3 to 5 minutes, until carrots are tender.

VARIATIONS
Carrot & Green Beans Sambhar or **Carrot & Zucchini Sambhar** are also great combinations. Use ½ cup of each vegetable.

Green Beans Sambhar

[Serves 4]

 Green beans are combined with tomatoes and spices in a wholesome lentil base. This sambhar is delicious served over plain rice or quinoa and as a dipping sauce with Uppuma (page 51), Dosais (page 52), or toasted naan.

½ cup masoor dal (red lentils) or moong dal (yellow lentils)

½ teaspoon ground turmeric divided

1 cup fresh green beans

2 tablespoons oil

¼ teaspoon asafoetida powder

2 to 4 curry leaves optional

1 whole dried red chili pepper

½ teaspoon black mustard seeds

½ teaspoon urad dal

½ cup onion slices cut lengthwise

½ cup chopped tomatoes

1 teaspoon sambhar powder

½ teaspoon salt more if desired

¼ teaspoon tamarind paste

¼ cup tomato sauce

1 tablespoon chopped fresh cilantro leaves

1 Bring 3 cups of water to a boil in a deep saucepan. Add masoor dal ro moong dal and ¼ teaspoon turmeric. Reduce heat to medium and cook, uncovered, for about 20 minutes, until dal becomes soft and creamy (if water evaporates during the cooking process, add another cup). Set aside.

2 Wash the green beans and cut off the ends. Cut each bean in half. Place in a bowl and set aside.

3 Heat oil in a saucepan over medium heat. When oil is hot, but not smoking, add asafoetida powder, curry leaves, red chili pepper, mustard seeds, and urad dal. Cover and cook until mustard seeds pop and urad dal turns golden brown, about 30 seconds.

4 Add onions, tomatoes, and green beans and cook for 1 minute.

5 Add remaining ¼ teaspoon turmeric, sambhar powder, and salt. Toss the seasonings well with the vegetables.

6 Add the cooked creamy dal, tamarind paste, and tomato sauce. Add 1 to 2 cups of warm water. (Sambhar can be thick or thin in consistency according to your taste, adjust the amount of water as you desire.) Stir and let mixture come to a boil.

7 Add cilantro and let mixture simmer for a few more minutes.

Kohlrabi Sambhar

[Serves 4]

 Kohlrabi is an often overlooked vegetable, but when cooked with lentils and spices as in this recipe, it becomes light, flavorful, and easy to prepare. This sambhar can be served over plain rice or quinoa and as a dipping sauce with Uppuma (page 51), Dosais (page 52), or toasted naan.

½ cup masoor dal (red lentils) or **moong dal (yellow lentils)**

½ **teaspoon ground turmeric** divided

2 tablespoons oil

¼ **teaspoon asafoetida powder**

1 whole dried red chili pepper

½ **teaspoon fenugreek seeds**

½ **teaspoon black mustard seeds**

½ **teaspoon urad dal**

¼ **cup chopped onions**

½ **cup chopped tomatoes**

1 cup peeled and thinly sliced kohlrabi

1 teaspoon sambhar powder

¼ **cup tomato sauce**

¼ **teaspoon tamarind paste**

1 teaspoon salt

1 tablespoon chopped fresh cilantro leaves

1 Bring 3 cups of water to a boil in a deep saucepan. Add masoor dal or moong dal and ¼ teaspoon turmeric. Reduce heat to medium and cook, uncovered, for about 20 minutes, until dal becomes creamy (if water evaporates during the cooking process, add up to another cup). Set aside.

2 In another saucepan, heat oil over medium heat. When oil is hot, but not smoking, add asafoetida powder, whole red chili pepper, fenugreek seeds, mustard seeds, and urad dal. Cook covered, until mustard seeds pop and urad dal is golden brown, about 30 seconds.

3 Stir in onions and tomatoes and cook 2 to 3 minutes, until onions are tender. Add kohlrabi and the remaining ¼ teaspoon turmeric. Stir well.

4 Add sambhar powder and tomato sauce. Stir and then add creamy dal mixture plus 2 cups of warm water. Stir well.

5 Add tamarind paste and salt. When mixture begins to bubble, reduce heat and cook kohlrabi until tender, 3 to 5 minutes.

6 Add cilantro and simmer for an additional few minutes.

Black-eyed Peas Kulambu

[Serves 4]

 This kulambu brings many textures and flavors together beautifully, including hearty black-eyed peas and tart mango in an aromatic delicious sauce. (Black-eyed Peas Kulambu can also be made nutritiously without a mango). You can serve this dish over rice or quinoa or enjoy it on its own as a nutritious soup.

2 tablespoons oil

¼ teaspoon asafoetida powder

1 whole dried red chili pepper

¼ teaspoon fenugreek seeds

½ teaspoon black mustard seeds

½ teaspoon urad dal

1 cup onion slices cut lengthwise

½ cup chopped tomatoes

¼ teaspoon ground turmeric

2 cups frozen black-eyed peas defrosted, or canned black-eyed peas rinsed and drained

2 teaspoons sambhar powder

½ teaspoon salt

1 cup tomato sauce

2 garlic cloves crushed

1 cup peeled and cubed un-ripe fresh mango cut into small cubes

1 tablespoon chopped fresh cilantro leaves

1 Place oil in a warmed saucepan. When oil is hot but not smoking, add asafoetida powder, red chili pepper, fenugreek seeds, mustard seeds, and urad dal. Stir over medium heat until mustard seeds pop and urad dal is golden brown, about 30 seconds.

2 Add onions and tomatoes and stir well. Add turmeric and cook until onions are translucent.

3 Add black-eyed peas, sambhar powder, and salt and stir. Add tomato sauce and 3 cups of warm water. When mixture begins to boil, add the crushed garlic and mango. Let simmer over low heat until black-eyed peas are tender.

4 Add chopped cilantro. Serve warm.

Okra Sambhar

[Serves 4]

Okra is a favorite vegetable in Indian cooking. It's also been traditionally enjoyed in the American south and is gaining in popularity across the country now. Okra are usually abundant in the summer but harder to find in winter months. When selecting okra choose tender okra and not the tough fibrous variety. You can use frozen cut okra for this recipe if you can't find fresh. The okra is cooked with tomatoes and onions in a seasoned lentil sauce. This delicious sambhar is best served over plain rice or quinoa.

½ cup masoor dal (red lentils) or moong dal (yellow lentils)

½ teaspoon ground turmeric divided

2 tablespoons oil

½ teaspoon asafoetida powder

1 whole dried red chili pepper

2 to 4 curry leaves optional

¼ teaspoon fenugreek seeds

½ teaspoon black mustard seeds

½ teaspoon urad dal

½ cup chopped onions

¼ cup chopped tomatoes

2 cups okra with tips removed and sliced into ½-inch pieces

2 teaspoons sambhar powder

¼ teaspoon tamarind paste

½ cup tomato sauce

1 teaspoon salt

1 Bring 3 cups of water to a boil in a deep saucepan over medium heat. Add masoor dal or moong dal and ¼ teaspoon turmeric. Reduce heat to medium and cook, uncovered, for about 20 minutes, until dal becomes creamy (if water evaporates during the cooking process, you may add up to another cup). Set aside.

2 Put oil in a saucepan, and put over medium heat. When oil is hot, but not smoking, add asafoetida powder, red chili pepper, curry leaves, fenugreek seeds, mustard seeds, and urad dal. Cover and cook over medium heat until mustard seeds pop and urad dal is golden brown, about 30 seconds.

3 Add onions and tomatoes and stir well. Add okra and the remaining ¼ teaspoon turmeric and sauté for 2 to 3 minutes over medium heat.

4 Add sambhar powder, tamarind paste, tomato sauce, and salt. Stir well.

5 Add cooked dal and about 2 cups of water and stir the mixture well. Let okra continue to cook over medium-low heat for 3 to 5 minutes.

Pearl Onion and Tomato Sambhar

[Serves 4]

 This classic aromatic sambhar is a popular dish in South India. This sambhar is delicious served over plain rice and as a dipping sauce with Uppuma (page 51), Dosais (page 52), or toasted naan.

½ cup masoor dal (red lentils) or moong dal (yellow lentils)

½ teaspoon ground turmeric divided

2 tablespoons oil

½ teaspoon asafoetida powder

2 to 4 curry leaves

1 whole dried red chili pepper

¼ teaspoon fenugreek seeds

½ teaspoon black mustard seeds

½ teaspoon urad dal

½ cup (about 12) fresh pearl onions peeled*

1 cup chopped tomatoes

2 teaspoons sambhar powder

1 teaspoon salt

½ cup tomato sauce

¼ teaspoon tamarind paste

1 tablespoon chopped fresh cilantro leaves

---

*Easy peeling instructions for pearl onions:
Boil the pearl onions in about 1 cup of water for about 45 seconds. Cool in cold water bath. Trim tips off onions and peel onions.

1 Bring 3 cups of water to a boil in a deep saucepan. Add masoor dal or moong dal and ¼ teaspoon turmeric. Reduce heat to medium and cook, uncovered, for about 20 minutes, until dal becomes creamy (if the water evaporates during the cooking process, add up to another cup). Set aside.

2 Place oil in a saucepan and heat over medium heat. When the oil is hot, but not smoking, add asafoetida powder, curry leaves, red chili pepper, fenugreek seeds, mustard seeds, and urad dal. Cook, covered, until mustard seeds pop and urad dal turns golden brown, about 30 seconds.

3 Add peeled pearl onions and tomatoes. Cover and cook, stirring often, for about 5 to 7 minutes, until onions are tender.

4 Add remaining ¼ teaspoon turmeric, sambhar powder, and salt and stir well with the onions and tomatoes. Cook, stirring, for 2 to 3 minutes.

5 Stir in tomato sauce, tamarind paste, cilantro, and 1 cup of warm water. Let onions cook in sauce over low heat, covered, for about 3 minutes.

6 Add the cooked dal and about 2 cups of warm water (making it the consistency you like). Cover and cook for 3 minutes. Add cilantro. Stir well and serve.

Zucchini Sambhar

[Serves 4]

 Zucchini, a favorite American summer squash, is used to prepare this delicious sambhar. Serve over plain rice or quinoa and as a dipping sauce with Uppuma (page 51), Dosais (page 52), or toasted naan.

½ cup masoor dal (red lentils) or **moong dal (yellow lentils)**

½ **teaspoon ground turmeric** divided

2 **tablespoons oil**

½ **teaspoon asafoetida powder**

1 **whole dried red chili pepper**

½ **teaspoon fenugreek seeds**

½ **teaspoon black mustard seeds**

½ **teaspoon urad dal**

½ **cup onion slices** cut lengthwise

½ **cup chopped tomatoes**

2 **teaspoons sambhar powder**

2 **cups peeled and cubed zucchini**

¼ **cup tomato sauce**

¼ **teaspoon tamarind paste**

1 **teaspoon salt** more, if desired

1 **tablespoon chopped fresh cilantro leaves**

1 Bring 3 cups of water to a boil in a deep saucepan. Add masoor dal or moong dal and ¼ teaspoon turmeric. Reduce heat to medium and cook, uncovered, for about 20 minutes, until dal becomes creamy (if water evaporates during the cooking process, add up to another cup). Set aside.

2 In another saucepan, heat oil over medium heat. When oil is hot, but not smoking, add asafoetida powder, red chili pepper, fenugreek seeds, mustard seeds, and urad dal. Cook, covered, until mustard seeds pop and urad dal is golden brown, about 30 seconds.

3 Add onions and tomatoes and cook 2 to 3 minutes, until onions are tender. Add remaining ¼ teaspoon turmeric and the sambhar powder and stir well.

4 Add zucchini and stir. Add cooked dal, tomato sauce, tamarind paste, and salt. When mixture begins to bubble, add 1½ cups of warm water. Stir, cover, and cook over low heat until zucchini is crisp-tender.

5 Add cilantro and simmer for an additional few minutes.

Vegetable Dishes

Asparagus with Shallots and Garlic

[Serves 4]

 Tender, sweet asparagus is a vegetable that is packed with flavor. This simple, quick side goes well with almost anything. You can toss it with quinoa or rice to create "Asparagus Quinoa" or "Asparagus Rice." A sure winner with kids too.

1 tablespoon oil

½ teaspoon black mustard seeds*

½ teaspoon urad dal*

2 shallots peeled and chopped

2 garlic cloves minced

1 pound asparagus trimmed and diced (about 2 cups)

½ teaspoon chutney powder**

¼ teaspoon salt

½ tablespoon grated fresh coconut or unsweetened shredded coconut

1 Heat oil in skillet over medium heat. When oil is hot but not smoking, add mustard seeds and urad dal. Stir until mustard seeds pop and urad dal turns golden, about 15 seconds.

2 Add chopped shallots and garlic. Stir and cook for 1 minute. Add asparagus and stir and cook for 2 minutes.

3 Add chutney powder, salt, and coconut. Stir gently.

*If you do not have black mustard seeds and urad dal, use cumin seeds.

**Instead of chutney powder you many use ½ teaspoon ground cumin.

Tender Asparagus with Ginger and Coconut

[Serves 4]

 This appealing dish combines a favorite spring vegetable, crisp asparagus, with red onions and coconut.

1 teaspoon oil

½ teaspoon black mustard seeds

½ teaspoon cumin seeds

¼ cup chopped red onions

½ tablespoon grated fresh ginger

1 teaspoon minced garlic cloves

1 pound asparagus sliced diagonally into about 1½-inch pieces (about 3 cups)

½ teaspoon ground cumin

¼ teaspoon salt more or less to taste

½ tablespoon grated fresh coconut or unsweetened dried coconut

1 Heat oil in a skillet over medium-high heat. When the oil is hot but not smoking, add mustard seeds and cumin seeds and stir until mustard seeds start to pop and cumin seeds change color to light brown, about 30 seconds.

2 Stir in onions, ginger, and garlic. Add asparagus and cook for 1 minute while stirring.

3 Stir in ground cumin and salt; cover and cook 3 to 5 minutes or until asparagus is tender but still crisp.

4 Add coconut, stir, and serve.

Sauteéd Baby Kale with Lentils and Coconut (Kale Poriyal)

[Serves 4]

 Organic baby kale is tender and mild in flavor and loaded with Vitamins A and C. This combination of kale and lentils works perfectly as a warm salad on its own, or as a side dish.

¼ cup yellow lentils (moong dal) rinsed and drained

¼ teaspoon ground turmeric

2 tablespoons oil

1 teaspoon mustard seeds

1 teaspoon urad dal

½ cup chopped onions

2 cloves garlic chopped

4 cups washed organic baby kale finely chopped*

½ teaspoon chutney powder

½ teaspoon salt

1 tablespoon unsweetened shredded coconut

---

*Boxed fresh baby kale can be found in the fresh salad section in the grocery store.

1 Bring 1 cup of water to a boil in a saucepan. Add dal and ¼ teaspoon turmeric and cook, uncovered, for about 15 minutes over medium heat until dal is semi-soft. Drain and set cooked dal aside.

2 Heat oil in a skillet over medium-high heat. When the oil is hot but not smoking, add mustard seeds and urad dal. Stir until mustard seeds start to pop and urad dal turns golden, about 15 seconds.

3 Add onions, and garlic, and stir for about 1 minute. Add chopped kale and cook for another minute while stirring.

4 Add chutney powder and salt. Stir and cook for 1 minute. Add cooked lentil to the above mixture and stir for 1 to 2 minutes. Add coconut. Toss and stir gently.

VARIATIONS

To make a delicious **Sautéed Baby Spinach with Lentils and Coconut (Spinach Poriyal)** substitute baby spinach for baby kale.

Stir-fried Beets with Coconut

[Serves 4]

 Not only are beets delicious, but they are loaded with nutrients like fiber, folate, and vitamin C. This flavorful stir-fry is a sure winner that will please any palate and makes a wonderful side dish.

3 cups peeled and evenly cubed beets (small cubes)

3 teaspoons oil

1 whole dried red chili pepper

2 to 4 curry leaves optional

½ teaspoon black mustard seeds

1 teaspoon urad dal

¼ teaspoon cayenne pepper powder

½ teaspoon ground cumin

½ teaspoon salt more if desired

¼ cup ground fresh coconut or unsweetened shredded coconut

1 Steam cubed beets in a steamer basket for 5 minutes until tender. Set aside.

2 Heat oil in a skillet over medium heat. When oil is hot, but not smoking, add dried red chili pepper and curry leaves. Stir in mustard seeds and urad dal. Cover until mustard seeds pop and urad dal is golden, about 15 seconds.

3 Add steamed beets to the skillet. Stir in cayenne pepper powder, ground cumin, and salt.

4 Cook and stir the beets with seasonings for a minute or two and serve garnished with shredded coconut.

Multicolored Bell Peppers in Lentil Sauce

[Serves 4]

 Multicolored bell peppers are cooked in a delicious lentil sauce with onions and tomatoes. This vegetable dish can be enjoyed with rice, bread, or as a side.

¼ cup masoor dal (red lentils) or **moong dal (yellow lentils)**

½ teaspoon ground turmeric divided

2 tablespoons oil

1 whole dried red chili pepper

4 to 6 curry leaves optional

¼ teaspoon asafoetida powder optional

½ teaspoon black mustard seeds

½ teaspoon urad dal

¼ cup chopped onions

¾ cup chopped tomatoes

2 cups diced multicolored bell peppers

½ teaspoon cayenne pepper powder

½ teaspoon ground cumin

¼ teaspoon tamarind paste optional

½ teaspoon salt

¼ cup tomato sauce

1 Bring about 2 cups of water to a boil in a saucepan. Add dal and ¼ teaspoon turmeric and cook for about 20 minutes over medium heat, uncovered, until dal is semi-soft. If water evaporates before dal is cooked, add an additional cup of water and heat until dal becomes soft. Set aside.

2 Heat oil in another saucepan over medium heat. When oil is hot, but not smoking, add red chili pepper, curry leaves, asafoetida powder, mustard seeds, and urad dal. Cover and fry over medium heat until mustard seeds pop and urad dal is golden brown, about 30 seconds.

3 Add onions, tomatoes, and remaining ¼ teaspoon turmeric and stir for a few minutes.

4 Add green bell peppers, cayenne, cumin, tamarind paste, and salt. Stir well. Add cooked dal, tomato sauce, and about ½ cup of warm water. Stir well. Cover and cook over medium heat until green peppers are tender.

Black-eyed Peas Masala

[Serves 4]

 This nutrition-packed, flavorful black-eyed peas dish is so satisfying! Serve with rice or quinoa or with any bread.

2 tablespoons oil

½ teaspoon black mustard seeds

½ teaspoon urad dal

½ cup chopped onions

½ cup chopped tomatoes

2 garlic cloves peeled and chopped

¼ teaspoon ground turmeric

2 teaspoons sambhar powder*

½ teaspoon salt

16 ounces frozen black-eyed peas thawed**

1 cup tomato sauce

1 Heat oil in a warm skillet over medium heat. When the oil is hot but not smoking, add mustard seeds and urad dal. Stir until mustard seeds pop and urad dal is golden, about 20 seconds.

2 Add onions, tomatoes, and garlic. Cook for 1 minute while stirring. Add ground turmeric, sambhar powder, and salt. Stir.

3 Add the thawed blackeyed peas and stir. Add tomato sauce and stir the mixture gently. Cover the skillet and let it cook over low-medium heat, stirring occasionally till the blackeyed peas are cooked. If needed add ¼ cup of water.

*You can substitute ½ teaspoon cayenne pepper powder and 1 teaspoon of ground cumin for sambhar powder.

**Instead of frozen black-eyed peas, you can use canned black-eyed peas—rinse, drain and follow the above recipe. Or you can use 1 cup of dried black-eyed peas boiled in 3 cups of water for approximately an hour until tender.

Broccoli with Coconut Stir-Fry (Poriyal)

[Serves 4]

 This is a South Indian twist on the usual broccoli stir-fry. Even if you're not fond of this vegetable, give this recipe a try—the flavors of chutney powder, mustard seeds, and coconut are sure to change your mind. It is an excellent nutritious side dish with any meal.

2 tablespoons oil

½ teaspoon black mustard seeds

1 teaspoon urad dal

¾ cup chopped onions

4 cups coarsely chopped broccoli including tender stems

1 teaspoon salt

1 teaspoon chutney powder

½ cup ground fresh coconut or unsweetened shredded coconut

Note: To enhance the dish, garnish with finely sliced red onions.

1 Heat oil in a large skillet over medium heat. When oil is hot but not smoking, stir in mustard seeds and urad dal. Cover and heat until mustard seeds pop and urad dal is golden brown, about 30 seconds.

2 Add onions and stir-fry for 30 seconds.

3 Add broccoli, salt, and chutney powder and stir well. Cover and cook for 5 to 7 minutes.

4 When the broccoli is tender but still crisp, add the coconut, stir well, and serve.

Cannellini Beans with Broccoli

[Serves 4]

 This combination of cannellini beans (white kidney beans) with broccoli is a colorful, buttery dish loaded with nutrition and taste! It's an extremely easy to prepare side dish that goes with any meal.

2 tablespoons oil

1 teaspoon black mustard seeds

1 teaspoon urad dal

1 cup chopped onions

4 cups chopped fresh broccoli (including tender stems)

1 teaspoon chutney powder

½ teaspoon salt or more, if desired

1 can (15-16 ounce) cannellini beans (or other white beans) drained and rinsed

1 Heat oil in a non-stick skillet. When oil is hot but not smoking, add mustard seeds and urad dal. Stir until mustard seeds start to pop and urad dal turns golden, about 20 seconds.

2 Add chopped onions and stir for 1 minute. Add broccoli and stir. Add chutney powder and salt and stir for 1 to 2 minutes.

3 Add cannellini beans and stir gently with broccoli for 1 minute. Remove from heat.

Brussels Sprouts with Chickpeas (Poriyal)

[Serves 4]

 A hearty and fiber-rich stir-fry dish, Brussels Sprouts with Chickpeas can be served as a salad, as a side dish with any meal, or it can be enjoyed as a delicious snack!

2 tablespoons oil

1 whole dried red chili pepper

½ teaspoon black mustard seeds

½ teaspoon urad dal

½ cup chopped onions

1 can (15 ounces) chickpeas rinsed and drained

3 cups coarsely chopped fresh Brussels sprouts

1 teaspoon salt

1 teaspoon chutney powder

½ cup ground fresh coconut or unsweetened shredded coconut

1 Heat oil in a skillet over medium heat. When oil is hot, but not smoking, stir in red chili pepper, mustard seeds, and urad dal. Cover and fry until mustard seeds pop and urad dal is golden brown, about 30 seconds.

2 Add onions and stir for 30 seconds. Add drained chickpeas. Stir, cover, and cook for about 2 minutes.

3 Add chopped Brussels sprouts, salt, and chutney powder and stir well. Cover and cook for 2 minutes over medium heat (be careful not to overcook the Brussels sprouts).

4 Add coconut. Mix well and cook for an additional minute.

 VARIATION
Use **4 cups chopped Brussels sprouts** without chickpeas to prepare plain **Brussels Sprout Stir-fry**.

Brussels Sprouts Masala

[Serves 4]

 Brussels sprouts cooked with garlic and tomatoes are an ideal option for those who enjoy cruciferous vegetables.

2 cups quartered Brussels sprouts

2 tablespoons oil

½ teaspoon black mustard seeds

½ teaspoon urad dal

½ cup chopped onions

1 cup chopped tomatoes

2 to 4 garlic cloves, chopped

¼ teaspoon ground turmeric

½ teaspoon cayenne pepper powder more, if desired

½ teaspoon ground cumin

½ teaspoon salt

½ cup tomato sauce

1 Steam Brussels sprouts until crisp tender. Set aside.

2 Place oil in a saucepan over medium heat. When oil is hot, but not smoking, add mustard seeds and urad dal and cover and fry until mustard seeds pop and urad dal turns golden, about 30 seconds.

3 Add onions, tomatoes, garlic, and turmeric and stir and cook until onions are tender.

4 Add cayenne, cumin, and salt. Cook for 1 minute. Add tomato sauce and stir well.

5 Add steamed Brussels sprouts and coat sprouts well with seasonings. Cover and cook over medium-low heat until Brussels sprouts are tender.

Cumin-Scented Butternut Squash

[Serves 4]

 What's not to like about butternut squash? It's packed with vitamins A and C, is rich in dietary fiber, and is delicious too. This winter squash is popular on holiday tables, and this recipe offers a tasty way to enjoy it with spices and coconut.

2 teaspoons oil

1 teaspoon black mustard seeds

½ teaspoon cumin seeds

½ medium onion sliced lengthwise (about ½ cup)

½ cup chopped tomatoes

½ teaspoon ground turmeric

½ teaspoon cayenne pepper powder more or less to taste

½ teaspoon ground cumin

¼ teaspoon salt more or less to taste

¼ cup tomato sauce

1 pound butternut squash peeled and cut in 1-inch cubes (about 2 cups)*

2 tablespoons chopped fresh cilantro

1 Heat oil in a skillet over medium-high heat. When the oil is hot but not smoking, add mustard seeds and cumin seeds and stir until mustard seeds start to pop, about 30 seconds.

2 Add onion and tomatoes and cook for 1 minute while stirring.

3 Add turmeric, cayenne, ground cumin, salt, and tomato sauce; stir and bring to a boil.

4 Add butternut squash, cover, and cook over medium heat for 5 to 7 minutes or until tender when pierced with a fork, adding water a tablespoon at a time if needed.

5 Add cilantro, gently stir and serve warm.

---

*Peeled pre-cut squash is available in some grocery stores.

Chickpeas with Ginger and Mango

[Serves 4]

 Protein-rich chickpeas paired with green mango and a zing of ginger makes a delectably healthy snack or side dish.

1 (15-ounce) can chickpeas

1 tablespoon oil

½ teaspoon black mustard seeds

½ teaspoon urad dal

¼ teaspoon ground turmeric

1 teaspoon chutney powder

1 teaspoon grated fresh ginger

¼ teaspoon salt more or less to taste

½ cup chopped fresh unripe peeled mango

1 teaspoon grated fresh coconut or
   unsweetened dried coconut

1 Drain chickpeas, rinse, and reserve.

2 Heat oil in a skillet over medium-high heat. When the oil is hot but not smoking, add black mustard seeds and urad dal and stir until mustard seeds start to pop and urad dal turns golden, about 30 seconds.

3 Add chickpeas, turmeric, chutney powder, ginger, and salt. Mix well. Cook over medium-low heat covered for 1 to 2 minutes.

4 Add mango. Stir over low heat for 1 minute.

5 Add coconut and stir the mixture gently. Serve warm.

 VARIATION
To make **Chickpeas with Ginger and Apple** substitute **½ cup unpeeled, diced green apple** for the mango.

Five-Color Vegetable Blend with Lentils

[Serves 4]

 This colorful, tasty vegetable blend makes a beautiful side dish. It can also be enjoyed as a salad or in a vegetable wrap.

1 tablespoon yellow lentils (moong dal)

2 tablespoons oil

¼ teaspoon asafoetida optional

½ teaspoon mustard seeds

1 teaspoon urad dal

½ cup chopped onions

¼ teaspoon ground turmeric

½ cup chopped green beans

½ teaspoon salt

½ cup shredded green cabbage

½ cup shredded red cabbage

½ cup chopped green bell pepper

1 teaspoon chutney or sambhar powder*

½ cup shredded carrots

1 tablespoon unsweetened shredded
   coconut

*You can use ¼ teaspoon cayenne pepper powder and ½ teaspoon ground cumin as a substitute for chutney powder or sambhar powder.

1 Soak moong dal in ½ cup water for 15 minutes. Drain water and set dal aside.

2 In a wide stainless steel skillet heat oil. When oil is hot but not smoking add asafoetida, mustard seeds and urad dal. Stir until mustard seeds start to pop, and urad dal turns golden, about 20 seconds. Stir in onions and cook for 1 minute. Add turmeric and stir.

3 Add green beans and salt. Stir and cook for about 3 minutes until beans are tender.

4 Add green cabbage, red cabbage, and green bell pepper. Add the drained moong dal and stir.

5 Add chutney (sambhar) powder. Add shredded carrots and stir for a couple of minutes until the vegetables are blended and crisp tender.

6 Add coconut and stir gently.

Spiced Spaghetti Squash

[Serves 4]

 Strands of spaghetti squash tossed with sautéed mustard seeds and cumin seeds and fragrant flavor-enhancing garam masala makes a unique, tasty side dish.

1 (3-pound) **spaghetti squash** (4 cups cooked)

1 tablespoon **oil**

1 teaspoon **black mustard seeds**

1 teaspoon **cumin seeds**

½ **cup chopped onions**

½ **fresh green chili pepper** minced (more or less to taste)

½ teaspoon **garam masala**

¼ **teaspoon salt** more or less to taste

¼ **cup chopped fresh cilantro**

2 **small whole dried red chili peppers** optional for garnish

1 To cook squash in microwave, cut in half lengthwise and remove seeds. Place cut side down in microwave and cook on high for 10 to 12 minutes or until soft. Let cool slightly.

2 Using a fork, pull the flesh lengthwise to separate it into long strands until you have 4 cups of squash. Save any additional squash for another time or freeze.

3 Heat oil in a skillet over medium-high heat. When the oil is hot but not smoking, add mustard seeds and cumin seeds and stir until mustard seeds start to pop and cumin seeds change color from light brown to semi-dark brown, about 30 seconds.

4 Add onions, chili pepper, garam masala, and salt. Sauté for 2 to 3 minutes until onions are tender. Add squash and toss to coat with the seasonings.

5 Place in serving dish and garnish with cilantro and red chili peppers, if using.

Cabbage in Lentil Sauce (Kootu)

[Serves 4]

 This is a lightly seasoned, creamy dish that is cooked with ginger. Serve as a side dish with any meal.

¾ cup masoor dal (red lentils) or **moong dal (yellow lentils)**

½ teaspoon ground turmeric divided

2 tablespoons oil

1 or 2 whole dried red chili peppers

2 or 3 curry leaves optional

½ teaspoon black mustard seeds

½ teaspoon urad dal

½ cup chopped onions

1 fresh green chili pepper minced (more, if desired)

1 tablespoon minced fresh ginger

2 cups coarsely shredded cabbage

1 teaspoon ground cumin

1 teaspoon salt

1 Bring 3 cups of water to a boil in a deep saucepan. Add masoor dal and ¼ teaspoon turmeric. Reduce heat to medium and cook dal, uncovered, until it becomes soft and tender, about 20 minutes (if most of the water evaporates before dal becomes soft, add an additional cup). Set aside.

2 Heat oil in a saucepan over medium heat. When oil is hot but not smoking, add whole red chili pepper, curry leaves, mustard seeds, and urad dal. Cover and cook until mustard seeds pop and urad dal is golden brown, about 30 seconds.

3 Add onions, chili pepper, and ginger. Stir well. Add cabbage and stir-fry about 1 minute.

4 Add remaining ¼ teaspoon turmeric, cumin, and salt and stir well. Immediately add cooked dal and about 1 cup of water. Cover and cook over medium heat for 5 to 7 minutes, stirring frequently so that cabbage is cooked and tender.

 VARIATION
To make **Cabbage and Carrot Kootu** use **1 cup shredded carrots** in place of one of the cups of cabbage.

Cabbage with Carrots Stir-Fry (Poriyal)

[Serves 4]

 This vibrant cabbage and carrot stir-fry can be served as a side dish or as a crispy, warm salad.

2 tablespoons oil

2 to 4 curry leaves optional

1 whole dried red chili pepper

½ teaspoon black mustard seeds

½ teaspoon urad dal

3 cups shredded cabbage

½ cup shredded carrots

½ fresh green chili pepper chopped

½ teaspoon minced fresh ginger

½ teaspoon salt more, if desired

1 tablespoon unsweetened shredded coconut

1 Place oil in a skillet over medium heat. When oil is hot, but not smoking, stir in curry leaves, red chili pepper, mustard seeds, and urad dal. Cover and fry until mustard seeds pop and urad dal is golden brown, about 30 seconds.

2 Add cabbage and carrots. Stir well and then stir in green chili pepper, ginger, and salt. Cover and cook over low heat until cabbage is crisp tender, about 2 to 3 minutes.

3 Add shredded coconut and stir well.

 VARIATIONS

To make **Cabbage and Green Peas Stir-fry** substitute **1 cup frozen green peas, thawed,** for the carrots.

To make **Plain Cabbage Stir-fry** delete carrots and use **3½ cups shredded cabbage.**

To make **Cabbage, Carrot & Farro Salad,** cook **1 cup farro** following package directions. In a bowl, drizzle farro with 1 tablespoon oil. Prepare the dish as above and toss with the farro.

Note: Any of the above cabbage stir-fries can also be enjoyed as a veggie wrap using wheat or flour tortillas. Warm the tortillas before filling with the stir-fry.

Seasoned Carrots with Coconut (Poriyal)

[Serves 4]

 A delightful stir-fry of carrots with coconut and mustard seeds that can be served as a side dish.

3 cups fresh carrots washed, peeled and sliced

1 tablespoon oil

4 to 6 curry leaves

1 whole dried red chili pepper

½ teaspoon black mustard seeds

½ teaspoon urad dal

½ teaspoon chutney powder

½ teaspoon salt

1 teaspoon unsweetened shredded coconut

1 Steam or microwave carrots in a small amount of water for about 5 minutes.

2 Place oil in a skillet over medium heat. When oil is hot, but not smoking, add curry leaves, red chili pepper, mustard seeds, and urad dal. Cover and fry until mustard seeds pop and urad dal turns golden brown, about 30 seconds.

3 Add carrots to the skillet and stir well with the seasonings. Add chutney powder and salt and stir well. Cook, covered, over medium-low heat until carrots are cooked according to your taste.

4 Mix coconut with carrots and serve.

Aloo Gobi

[Serves 4]

 Aloo Gobi is a standard North Indian vegetable dish that is served in most Indian restaurants. Here is a simple, lighter version of Aloo Gobi, a delightful combination of potatoes and cauliflower!

1 cup peeled and cubed potatoes (small pieces)

2 cups small cauliflower florets

3 tablespoons oil

¼ teaspoon cumin seeds

1 cup chopped onions

5 garlic cloves chopped

1 tablespoon shredded ginger

½ teaspoon ground turmeric

½ teaspoon cayenne pepper powder or more, if desired

1 teaspoon ground cumin

½ teaspoon salt or more, if desired

1 tablespoon cilantro finely chopped

1 Place potatoes in a steam basket in a saucepan filled with two inches of water. Bring water to a boil. Cover and steam until fork tender. Allow potatoes to cool. Set aside.

2 Place cauliflower florets in the same steam basket and steam for about 3 minutes until crisp tender. Set aside.

3 Heat oil in a skillet. When oil is hot, but not smoking, add the cumin seeds and stir for about 20 seconds. Immediately add the onions, garlic, and ginger. Sauté for 2 minutes over medium heat.

4 Add ground turmeric and stir. Add the steamed vegetables to the skillet. Gently stir in cayenne pepper powder, ground cumin, and salt.

5 Cook over low heat, stirring gently, for about 3 to 5 minutes. Garnish with cilantro.

Cauliflower in Lentil Sauce (Kootu)

[Serves 4]

 Delightfully seasoned cauliflower cooked with ginger in lentil sauce makes a great nutritious side dish!

¾ cup moong dal (yellow lentils)

½ teaspoon ground turmeric divided

2 tablespoons oil

1 whole dried red chili pepper

2 to 4 curry leaves optional

½ teaspoon black mustard seeds

½ teaspoon urad dal

¼ cup chopped onions

1 tablespoon minced fresh ginger

1 teaspoon finely chopped fresh green chili pepper

2 cups cauliflower pieces cut into small florets

½ teaspoon ground cumin

½ teaspoon salt

1 tablespoon chopped cilantro

1 Bring 4 cups of water to a boil in a saucepan. Add moong dal and ¼ teaspoon turmeric. Reduce heat to medium and cook, uncovered, for about 30 minutes, until dal is tender and creamy (if water evaporates during the cooking process, add another cup). Set aside.

2 Heat oil in a saucepan over medium heat. When oil is hot, but not smoking, add red chili pepper, curry leaves, mustard seeds, and urad dal. Cover and cook until mustard seeds pop and urad dal turns golden brown, about 30 seconds.

3 Add onions, ginger, green chili pepper, and remaining ¼ teaspoon turmeric. Stir well.

4 Add cauliflower and coat well with the seasonings.

5 Add reserved cooked dal, cumin, salt, and about ½ cup warm water. Stir cauliflower well with the dal mixture for a minute or two. Cover and cook over low heat until cauliflower is just tender, 2 to 4 minutes.

6 Add cilantro and gently mix with cauliflower.

Cauliflower Masala

[Serves 4]

 This cauliflower stir-fry with onions, tomatoes, and spices makes a colorful and tasty side dish.

3 cups cauliflower pieces cut in 1-inch to 1½-inch chunks including short stems

2 tablespoons oil

½ teaspoon black mustard seeds

½ teaspoon urad dal

½ cup chopped onions

½ cup chopped tomatoes

2 or 3 garlic cloves chopped

¼ teaspoon ground turmeric

½ teaspoon cayenne pepper powder more, if desired

½ teaspoon ground cumin

½ cup tomato sauce

1 teaspoon salt

1 Steam the cauliflower pieces until crisp-tender. Set aside.

2 Heat oil in a skillet over medium heat. When oil is hot, but not smoking, add mustard seeds and urad dal. Cover and cook until mustard seeds pop and urad dal is golden brown, about 30 seconds.

3 Add onions, tomatoes, and garlic. Stir-fry for 1 minute over medium heat.

4 Add turmeric, cayenne, and cumin. Stir well over medium heat for 1 minute. Add tomato sauce and salt. Mix well to obtain a thick paste-like consistency.

5 Add steamed cauliflower pieces and stir carefully to coat with sauce. Cook uncovered over medium heat for about 2 minutes. Be careful not to overcook!

Cauliflower, Potato and Green Peas Medley

[Serves 4]

 This mixed vegetable stir-fry is popular in South India. It can be served as a side dish or as a filler in a veggie wrap.

1 cup cauliflower florets

2 tablespoons oil

2 to 4 curry leaves optional

½ teaspoon mustard seeds

½ teaspoon urad dal

½ cup chopped onions

1 cup chopped tomatoes

2 garlic cloves chopped

1 cup peeled and cubed potatoes

¼ teaspoon ground turmeric

½ teaspoon cayenne pepper powder

½ teaspoon ground cumin

½ teaspoon salt

½ cup frozen green peas thawed

1 Steam the cauliflower florets in a steam basket until crisp-tender. Set aside.

2 Put oil in skillet over medium heat. When oil is hot, but not smoking, add curry leaves, mustard seeds, and urad dal. Cover and fry until mustard seeds pop and urad dal turns golden brown, about 30 seconds.

3 Add onions, tomatoes, and garlic and sauté for a few minutes.

4 Add potatoes and stir well. Add turmeric, cayenne, cumin, and salt and stir the seasonings with the potatoes. Add 2 tablespoons of water and cover and cook over low-medium heat until potatoes are partially cooked.

5 Stir in steamed cauliflower. Cook, uncovered, for about 1 minute.

6 Stir in thawed green peas and cook briefly.

Chana Masala

[Serves 4]

 Chana Masala (spiced chickpeas) is a popular Indian dish that you'll often find on Indian restaurant menus. Protein and fiber-rich chickpeas (garbanzo beans) are cooked in a zesty ginger-garlic sauce with spices. Enjoy with breads or as a side dish.

1 tablespoon oil

1 bay leaf

2 slivers cinnamon sticks

½ teaspoon cumin seeds

1 (15-ounce) can chickpeas rinsed and drained

1 teaspoon lemon juice

¼ cup chopped cilantro

For ground spice paste:

1 tablespoon oil

2 slivers cinnamon sticks

½ teaspoon cumin seeds

½ cup chopped red onions

3 garlic cloves

2 thick slices ginger

8 whole cashews

¼ teaspoon ground turmeric

½ teaspoon cayenne pepper powder

¼ teaspoon ground cardamom

½ teaspoon garam masala

1 cup chopped tomatoes

1 cup warm water

1 Prepare the ground spice paste: Heat oil in a skillet. When oil is warm add cinnamon sticks and cumin seeds and stir for 15 seconds. Add onions, garlic, ginger and cashews and stir for 1 minute. Add turmeric, cayenne pepper powder, ground cardamom, and garam masala. Stir and cook for 1 minute. Add chopped tomatoes. Stir and cook for 1 to 2 minutes. Cool and transfer the ingredients in the skillet to a blender. Add 1 cup of warm water and blend to a smooth paste. Set aside.

2 Heat oil in a wide saucepan. When oil is hot but not smoking, add bay leaf, cinnamon stick slivers, and cumin seeds. Stir for 15 seconds. Add drained chickpeas and stir for about a minute.

3 Gently stir in the ground spice paste over low-medium heat.

4 Add lemon juice and salt to the saucepan. Stir and cook on low heat for about 5 minutes, gently mashing a few chickpeas as they cook. This process allows the sauce to thicken and bind well.

5 Cook for additional 2 minutes in low heat. Add cilantro and stir.

Seasoned Baby Eggplant Stir-fry

[Serves 4]

 Baby eggplants are available at farmer's market in Summer and Fall. They are also available throughout the year in Indian, Mexican and Thai groceries. Here, baby eggplants are cooked in a light and tasty combination of seasonings to make an excellent accompaniment to any meal.

6 to 8 baby eggplants

3 tablespoons oil

2 to 4 curry leaves

½ teaspoon black mustard seeds

½ teaspoon urad dal

½ cup sliced onions cut lengthwise

¼ cup chopped tomatoes

2 to 4 garlic cloves peeled and chopped

½ teaspoon ground turmeric

½ teaspoon cayenne pepper powder

½ teaspoon ground cumin

½ teaspoon salt

¼ cup tomato sauce

1 Wash the baby eggplants and dry them with paper towels. Remove stems and quarter them lengthwise. Set aside.

2 In a non-stick skillet, heat oil. When oil is hot but not smoking, add curry leaves, mustard seeds, and urad dal. Let mustard seeds crackle and urad dal turn golden, about 15 seconds.

3 Add onions, garlic, and turmeric and sauté for 1 to 2 minutes. Add quartered eggplant and stir for 2 minutes.

4 Add cayenne pepper powder, ground cumin, and salt. Stir and mix the seasonings with eggplant. Add tomato sauce and stir. Close the skillet and cook on low-medium heat for 4 to 6 minutes, until eggplants becomes soft and tender. Gently stir.

Eggplant and Potato Masala

[Serves 4]

 Potatoes pair well with eggplant. Here is a delightful combination that can be served as a side dish. It goes especially well with Fragrant Lemon Rice (page 77).

6 baby eggplants or ½ large eggplant

1 cup peeled and cubed potatoes cut lengthwise 1½ x ½ inches

3 tablespoons oil

1 teaspoon cumin seeds

½ cup sliced onions cut lengthwise

1 cup chopped tomatoes

½ teaspoon ground turmeric

½ teaspoon cayenne pepper powder

½ teaspoon ground cumin

½ teaspoon salt

¼ teaspoon garam masala

1 cup tomato sauce

1 tablespoon unsweetened shredded coconut

1 Cut unpeeled eggplant(s) into pieces the same size as potatoes to make about 2 cups.

2 Place oil in a heavy skillet over medium heat. When oil is hot but not smoking, add cumin seeds. Cover and cook until seeds are golden brown.

3 Add onions and tomatoes and stir-fry for a few minutes.

4 Add potatoes and turmeric. Mix well, cover, and cook over medium heat, stirring often, for 3 to 5 minutes, until potatoes are slightly cooked.

5 Add eggplant and mix well. Add cayenne, ground cumin, salt, garam masala, and tomato sauce and mix well. (You may add about 2 tablespoons of water at this point to facilitate the cooking process.) Cover and cook over medium-low heat until vegetables are tender.

6 Add coconut and gently stir.

Indian Ratatouille

[Serves 4]

 Ratatouille is a popular dish from the Provence region of France. Here is my take with Indian flavors! Beautiful purple eggplant and green zucchini are cooked with garlic and tomatoes in this mildly spiced version. This dish can be enjoyed on its own or as a side dish. It can also be served on toasted bread as an appetizer (bruschetta).

3 tablespoons olive oil

½ teaspoon cumin seeds

½ cup finely chopped onion

¼ cup finely chopped tomatoes

3 cloves garlic chopped

2 cups peeled eggplant coarsely chopped (about ¾-inch cubes)

1 cup green zucchini cut into ¼-inch thick slices

½ teaspoon salt

¼ teaspoon ground turmeric

½ teaspoon garam masala

½ teaspoon cayenne pepper powder

½ cup tomato sauce

1 Place oil in a skillet over medium heat. When oil is hot but not smoking, stir in cumin seeds to brown, about 20 seconds. Add onions, tomatoes, and garlic. Stir-fry for about 2 minutes.

2 Add eggplant, zucchini, and salt. Cook covered over medium heat, stirring often, for 3 to 5 minutes, until vegetables are slightly cooked.

3 Add turmeric, garam masala, cayenne pepper powder, and stir. Add tomato sauce and mix well. Cover and cook over low heat until eggplant and zucchini are cooked soft.

Green Beans in Lentil Sauce (Kootu)

[Serves 4]

 This is one of my favorite ways to enjoy green beans—with lentils in a creamy sauce. It is a soothing side dish!

½ cup masoor dal (red lentils) or moong dal (yellow lentils)

¼ teaspoon ground turmeric

2 tablespoons oil

½ teaspoon black mustard seeds

½ teaspoon urad dal

½ cup chopped onions

½ fresh green chili pepper

1 tablespoon minced fresh ginger

3 cups chopped green beans about ½-inch pieces

½ teaspoon ground cumin

½ teaspoon salt more if desired

1 Bring 2 cups of water to a boil in a deep saucepan. Add masoor dal or moong dal and turmeric. Reduce heat to medium and cook dal, uncovered, until it becomes creamy, about 20 minutes. (If water evaporates before dal becomes soft, add up to an additional 1 cup of water.) Set aside.

2 Heat oil in a saucepan over medium heat. When oil is hot but not smoking, add mustard seeds and urad dal. Cover and cook until mustard seeds pop and urad dal is golden brown, about 30 seconds.

3 Add onions, chili pepper, and ginger. Stir well. Add cut green beans and stir-fry for about 3 minutes.

4 Stir in ground cumin and salt. Immediately add cooked dal and about 1 cup of warm water. Cover and cook over medium heat for 3 to 5 minutes, stirring frequently so that beans are cooked and tender.

VARIATION
To make a soothing **Eggplant in Lentil Sauce**, follow the above recipe using **3 cups of cubed (½-inch pieces) unpeeled eggplant** in place of the green beans.

Seasoned Green Beans with Coconut

[Serves 4]

 A simple, easy-to-prepare version of stir-fried green beans flavored with coconut!

2 teaspoons oil

1 whole dried red chili pepper

½ teaspoon black mustard seeds

½ teaspoon urad dal

3 cups chopped green beans about ½-inch
   pieces

½ teaspoon cayenne pepper powder

1 teaspoon minced fresh ginger

½ teaspoon salt more, if desired

1 tablespoon unsweetened shredded
   coconut

1 Heat oil in a skillet over medium heat. When oil is hot, but not smoking, add red chili pepper, mustard seeds, and urad dal. Cover and fry briefly until mustard seeds pop and urad dal turns golden brown, about 30 seconds.

2 Add green beans to skillet and mix with the seasonings. Add cayenne pepper powder, ginger, and salt. Cover and cook over low-medium heat until green beans are tender.

3 Stir in coconut. Serve warm.

Vibrant Green Beans and Carrot Stir-fry (Poriyal)

[Serves 4 to 6]

 This vibrant, colorful stir-fry is a perfect way to enjoy two favorite vegetables that will please any palate.

2 tablespoons oil

1 whole dried red chili pepper more or less to taste

1 teaspoon black mustard seeds

1 teaspoon urad dal

2 cups chopped green beans about ½-inch pieces

2 cups peeled and chopped carrots about ½-inch pieces, steamed

1 teaspoon grated fresh ginger

½ teaspoon cayenne pepper powder

¼ teaspoon salt more or less to taste

2 tablespoons grated fresh coconut or unsweetened dried coconut

1 Heat oil in a skillet over medium-high heat. When the oil is hot but not smoking, add red chili pepper, mustard seeds, and urad dal. Stir until mustard seeds pop and urad dal turns golden, about 30 seconds.

2 Add green beans and steamed carrots and stir-fry for about 1 minute.

3 Stir in ginger, cayenne pepper powder, and salt. Add 1 tablespoon water, cover, and cook on medium to low heat until vegetables are tender but still crisp, about 2 to 3 minutes.

4 Add coconut, stir and serve.

Green Bean and Yellow Lentil Stir-fry (Poriyal)

[Serves 4]

 This fiber rich, colorful side dish features green beans with yellow lentils and ginger. Because of the green and gold color combination, I refer to this dish as a "Green Bay Packers Stir-fry"!

¼ **cup moong dal (yellow lentils)***

¼ **teaspoon ground turmeric**

2 **tablespoons oil**

2 **or 3 curry leaves** optional

½ **teaspoon black mustard seeds**

1 **teaspoon urad dal**

1 **pound green beans** stems removed and diced about ½ inch long (about 3 cups)

1 **teaspoon minced fresh ginger**

½ **fresh green chili pepper** finely chopped (optional)

½ **teaspoon salt** more, if desired

½ **teaspoon cayenne pepper powder**

1 **tablespoon unsweetened shredded coconut**

---

*You can use yellow split peas instead of moong dal. But the cooking time in Step 1 will be about 30 minutes.

1 Bring 2 cups of water to a boil in a saucepan. Add moong dal and turmeric. Cook over medium heat, uncovered, for about 20 minutes, until dal is tender but not creamy. (If water evaporates before dal becomes tender add up to an additional ½ cup of water.) Drain and set aside.

2 Heat oil in a large skillet over medium heat. When oil is hot, but not smoking, stir in curry leaves, mustard seeds, and urad dal. Cover and heat until mustard seeds pop and urad dal is golden brown, about 30 seconds.

3 Add green beans, ginger, and green chili pepper and stir well. Cook over medium heat for about 1 minute.

4 Add salt and cayenne pepper powder and mix well. Cover beans and cook over low heat for 5 to 7 minutes. (*Note:* a sprinkle or two of water may, however, be added on top of the green beans to facilitate the cooking process.)

5 When beans are tender but still crisp, add cooked moong dal and shredded coconut. Stir well. Serve immediately or remove from heat and keep covered until serving time. Be careful not to overcook beans.

Lentil Crumble with Coconut

[Serves 4]

 This delicious, textured side dish made from split peas is rich in heart-healthy soluble fiber.

½ cup yellow split peas

2 whole dried red chili peppers

1½ teaspoons cumin seeds divided

1 teaspoon fennel seeds

3 tablespoons oil

1 teaspoon black mustard seeds

1 cup chopped onions

½ teaspoon ground turmeric

¼ teaspoon cayenne pepper powder more
   or less to taste

½ teaspoon salt more or less to taste

2 tablespoons chopped cilantro

2 tablespoons grated fresh coconut or
   unsweetened dried coconut

1 Place split peas in a bowl and cover with hot water. Let soak for 30 minutes.

2 Drain the split peas and put in a blender or food processor with red chili peppers, 1 teaspoon cumin seeds, fennel seeds, and ¼ cup of warm water. Blend or process until the texture of coarse cornmeal. Pour mixture into a microwave-safe dish, cover with a small plate, and cook on high for 3 minutes—mixture will feel somewhat firm. Cool for 5 minutes and then break into small pieces with a fork. Reserve the crumble.

3 Heat oil in a skillet over medium-high heat. When the oil is hot but not smoking, add black mustard seeds and remaining ½ teaspoon cumin seeds and stir until mustard seeds start to pop and cumin seeds change color from light brown to semi-dark brown.

4 Add onions and cook for 30 seconds while stirring.

5 Add reserved split pea crumble mixture, turmeric, cayenne, and salt. Continue to cook over medium-low heat for 2 to 4 minutes, while stirring, until the split pea crumble becomes golden and grainy in texture.

6 Add cilantro and coconut, stir and serve.

Matar Paneer

[Serves 4]

"Matar" is the Hindi word for "green peas." Green peas with paneer (Indian cheese) is an unbeatable and delicious combination. Ready-made paneer is available in Indian grocery stores. This dish is commonly served in Indian restaurants. Our's is a simplified version of this popular North Indian dish. It's delicious with any bread or with rice, and can also be served as a side dish.

2 tablespoons oil

2 slivers cinnamon stick

1 bay leaf

½ teaspoon cumin seeds

¼ teaspoon ground turmeric

1 teaspoon garam masala

1 teaspoon ground cumin

½ teaspoon cayenne pepper powder more if desired

½ teaspoon salt

1 cup warm water

½ cup tomato sauce

1 cup frozen green peas thawed

7 ounces paneer cubed*

¼ cup cilantro chopped

For ground paste:

1 tablespoon oil

1 cup chopped onions

3 cloves garlic

10 whole cashews

1 tablespoon sliced ginger

1 cup chopped tomatoes

---

*Paneer is available in Indian grocery stores and one package is about 14 ounces. Use only about half (7 ounces) from the package. Cut the paneer into small ½-inch cubes. Leftover paneer can be stored in the freezer for later use.

1 Make the ground paste: Heat the oil in a non-stick skillet. Add onions, garlic, cashews, ginger, and tomatoes. Stir and cook till onions are translucent. Cool the ingredients. Now transfer the ingredients to a blender. Add 1 cup of water and grind to a paste. Set aside.

2 Heat oil in wide saucepan. When oil is hot but not smoking, add cinnamon stick slivers, bay leaf and cumin seeds. Stir. Add the ground paste and stir the seasonings with the paste.

3 Add turmeric, garam masala, ground cumin, cayenne pepper powder, and salt. Blend with the paste. Add about 1 cup of warm water and ½ cup tomato sauce. Stir, cover, and cook for 3 to 5 minutes.

4 Add green peas and cubed paneer. If the mixture gets thick you can dilute it with about ½ cup of warm water. Stir, cover, and cook for 3 to 5 minutes. Add cilantro. Stir and mix gently.

VARIATION

To make a delicious **Matar Tofu**, substitute cubed firm tofu for paneer in this recipe.

Heavenly Lima Beans Masala

[Serves 4 to 6]

 Protein rich lima beans cooked with seasonings and tomato sauce makes a heavenly side dish. It can also be enjoyed as a veggie wrap with warmed tortillas or as a filling for pita bread.

1 package (16 ounces) frozen baby lima
    beans thawed (about 2½ cups)

3 tablespoons oil

2 or 3 (½-inch-long) slivers cinnamon stick

½ teaspoon black mustard seeds

½ teaspoon urad dal

½ cup chopped onions

½ cup chopped tomatoes

½ teaspoon ground turmeric

½ teaspoon cayenne pepper powder more
    if desired

½ teaspoon ground cumin

1 teaspoon salt

1 cup tomato sauce

2 tablespoons unsweetened shredded dried
    coconut

1 Bring ¾ cup of water to a boil in a saucepan. Add lima beans and return to boil. Reduce heat to medium, cover, and cook on low heat for 5 to 7 minutes, stirring occasionally. Set aside.

2 Place oil in a skillet over medium heat. When oil is hot, but not smoking, add slivers of cinnamon stick, mustard seeds, and urad dal. Cover and cook over medium heat until mustard seeds pop and urad dal is golden brown, about 30 seconds.

3 Add onions and tomatoes and stir for a few minutes. Add turmeric and stir well over medium heat. Add cayenne, cumin, and salt and stir well for 1 minute. Add tomato sauce.

4 When mixture begins to boil, add undrained cooked lima beans and stir well. Cover and cook over medium heat until lima beans are tender.

5 Add coconut and stir well.

Lima Beans and Coconut Stir-fry

[Serves 4]

 Even if you dislike lima beans, you will be in for a pleasant surprise when you try this dish. Packed with protein and fiber, this is an easy-to-prepare stir-fry that is a great side dish as well as a healthy snack.

1 package (10 to 16 ounces) frozen baby or Fordhook (large) lima beans

2 tablespoons oil

2 to 4 curry leaves optional

1 whole dried red chili pepper

½ teaspoon black mustard seeds

½ teaspoon urad dal

1 teaspoon chutney powder*

1 teaspoon salt

1 tablespoon unsweetened shredded coconut

_____

* You may try substituting ½ teaspoon cayenne pepper powder for the 1 teaspoon chutney powder for a slightly different taste.

1 Cook lima beans in microwave or on stovetop according to package direction. Drain and set side.

2 Place oil in a skillet over medium heat. When oil is hot, but not smoking, stir in curry leaves, red chili pepper, mustard seeds, and urad dal. Cover and fry until mustard seeds pop and urad dal is golden brown, about 30 seconds.

3 Add drained lima beans and stir-fry for a few minutes over medium heat.

4 Add chutney powder and salt and stir to coat the lima beans with the seasonings. Add shredded coconut, stir, and serve warm.

Mushroom Cashew Kurma

[Serves 4]

 Sliced mushrooms are cooked in a delicious coconut- and cashew-based sauce. This vegan kurma can be served with naan or warm whole wheat tortillas. It can also be enjoyed over plain rice or even over angel hair or any other pasta.

2 tablespoons oil

1 bay leaf

2 to 4 slivers of cinnamon stick

½ teaspoon cumin seeds

1 cup chopped red onions

¼ teaspoon ground turmeric

3 cups sliced white mushrooms

¼ teaspoon garam masala

½ teaspoon cayenne pepper powder

½ teaspoon salt more if desired

For ground paste:

¼ cup unsweetened shredded coconut

1 teaspoon fennel seeds

1 tablespoon sliced ginger

1 clove garlic, peeled

¼ cup raw or roasted cashew halves

¼ cup chopped tomatoes

1 cup warm water

1 Make the ground paste: Grind coconut, fennel seeds, ginger, garlic, cashews, and tomatoes with warm water in a blender to a smooth paste. Set aside.

2 Heat oil in a wide-bottomed saucepan. When oil is hot but not smoking, add bay leaf, cinnamon stick slivers and cumin seeds. When cumin seeds are lightly browned, add onions and stir in with turmeric.

3 Add mushrooms and stir for 2 minutes over medium heat.

4 Add garam masala, cayenne pepper powder, and salt and stir for a minute. Add the ground paste and 1 cup of warm water. Stir and cook for 5 to 7 minutes over low heat.

 VARIATION
To prepare an absolutely delicious **Mushroom and Green Peas Cashew Kurma** add ½ **cup of frozen green peas** (thawed) in step 4.

Mushroom Masala

[Serves 4]

 Lightly seasoned mushrooms cooked with onions and tomatoes make a delicious side dish!

1 teaspoon oil

½ teaspoon cumin seeds

½ cup chopped onions

¼ cup chopped tomatoes

1 tablespoon tomato sauce

¼ teaspoon cayenne pepper powder

½ teaspoon ground cumin

½ teaspoon salt

2 cups (8 ounces) white button mushrooms
    cut in half

1 Place oil in a skillet over medium heat. When oil is hot, but not smoking, add cumin seeds and cook for about 30 seconds. Immediately add the onions and tomatoes and stir-fry for a few minutes.

2 Add tomato sauce, cayenne, ground cumin, and salt. When the mixture thickens, add mushrooms and stir well. Cook mushrooms, uncovered, on low heat for 3 minutes.

Okra Masala (Bhindi Masala)

[Serves 4]

 Lightly seasoned and simmered with tomatoes and spices, this okra is a favorite in Indian cuisine. Okra Masala (also known as Bhindi Masala) goes well with any flavored or plain rice dish.

2 tablespoons oil

¼ teaspoon asafoetida powder optional

½ teaspoon black mustard seeds

½ teaspoon urad dal

½ cup chopped onions

½ cup chopped tomatoes

½ teaspoon ground turmeric

½ teaspoon cayenne pepper powder

½ teaspoon ground cumin

½ cup tomato sauce

1 teaspoon salt

3 cups sliced fresh okra or thawed frozen cut okra

1 Place oil in skillet over medium heat. When oil is hot, but not smoking, add asafoetida powder, mustard seeds, and urad dal. Cover and fry until mustard seeds pop and urad dal turns golden brown, about 30 seconds.

2 Add onions and tomatoes and stir-fry for 1 minute. Add turmeric, cayenne, cumin, tomato sauce, and salt. Cook for 1 to 2 minutes.

3 Add okra and stir-fry for 3 to 5 minutes. Cover and cook over low heat until okra is tender.

4 Gently stir for an additional minute and serve.

Parsnips with Green Peas

[Serves 4]

 Parsnips are a root vegetable related to carrots and parsley and they are loaded with nutrients too! Parsnips have cream-colored skin and the flesh has a mild, sweet flavor. This is a colorful side dish that even kids would love.

2 cups washed, peeled, and cubed parsnips

2 tablespoons oil

1 teaspoon cumin seeds

¼ teaspoon cayenne pepper powder

¼ teaspoon salt

1 cup frozen petite green peas thawed

1 Place cubed parsnips in a steam basket and steam for 3 to 5 minutes. Set aside.

2 Heat oil in a non-stick skillet. When oil is warm, add cumin seeds. Immediately add steamed parsnips and stir. Add cayenne pepper and salt. Stir.

3 Add thawed peas and slowly stir the vegetables until heated through.

Potatoes in Lentil Sauce

[Serves 4]

 The delicate flavors of the spices and tomatoes bring this potato lentil dish to life. It's like having dal but with the extra heartiness of potatoes added. Serve over plain rice or quinoa, or with naan bread.

½ cup moong dal (yellow lentils)

¾ teaspoon ground turmeric divided

1 cup scrubbed and cubed potatoes (about 1½-inch cubes)

3 tablespoons oil

1 whole dried red chili pepper

1 teaspoon cumin seeds

½ cup chopped onions

1 cup chopped tomatoes

1 teaspoon ground cumin

½ teaspoon cayenne pepper powder more or less to taste

¼ teaspoon salt more or less to taste

½ cup chopped fresh cilantro

1 Bring 3 cups of water to a boil in a 1-quart saucepan. Add moong dal and ¼ teaspoon turmeric. Reduce heat to medium and cook, uncovered, for about 30 minutes, until dal softens (if water evaporates during the cooking process, add another ½ cup). Do not drain. Mash moong dal with potato masher. Reserve.

2 Parboil the potatoes until partially cooked. Drain and set aside.

3 Heat oil in a skillet over medium-high heat. When the oil is hot but not smoking, add red chili pepper and cumin seeds. Stir until cumin seeds change color from light brown to semi-dark brown, about 30 seconds.

4 Add onions, tomatoes, ground cumin, cayenne, and remaining ½ teaspoon turmeric. Cook about 2 to 3 minutes or until onions are tender.

5 Add reserved mashed moong dal, parboiled potatoes, salt, and cilantro; stir to combine. Bring to a simmer. Reduce heat to low and simmer about 3 to 5 minutes until potatoes are tender, stirring occasionally and adding up to ½ cup of warm water, if needed.

Potatoes in Almond Coconut Sauce (Potato Kurma)

[Serves 4]

Potatoes cooked in a delectable coconut and almond-based sauce, Potato Kurma can be served over plain rice, with a rice pilaf, with naan or plain toasted bread, or with warm whole wheat tortillas.

½ cup unsweetened shredded coconut

2 fresh green chili peppers more, if desired

16 raw almonds

2 teaspoons cumin seeds divided

1 teaspoon fennel seeds divided

2 thick slices fresh ginger

1 tablespoon oil

1 tablespoon unsalted butter

2 to 4 curry leaves optional

1 bay leaf

2 to 4 (½-inch-long) slivers cinnamon sticks

1 cup coarsely chopped onions

2 cups chopped tomatoes divided

2 cups peeled and cubed Idaho potatoes
    (about 1-inch cubes)

½ teaspoon ground turmeric

1 teaspoon curry powder

1 teaspoon salt more, if desired

¼ cup chopped fresh cilantro leaves

1 In a blender put coconut, green chili peppers, almonds, 1 teaspoon cumin seeds, ½ teaspoon fennel seeds, ginger, and 2 cups hot water. Grind into a smooth paste.

2 Place oil and butter in a wide-bottomed saucepan over medium heat. When oil is hot but not smoking, add curry leaves, bay leaf, cinnamon sticks, remaining 1 teaspoon cumin seeds, and remaining ½ teaspoon fennel seeds. Stir-fry to a golden brown.

3 Add onions and 1 cup chopped tomatoes and stir-fry for a few minutes.

4 Add potatoes and turmeric and stir well for 1 minute. Add curry powder and stir the seasonings well with potatoes for couple of minutes.

5 Add the coconut spice paste from the blender along with salt and 2 cups of warm water and mix thoroughly.

6 When mixture begins to boil, add the remaining 1 cup of chopped tomatoes and cook over medium heat until potatoes are tender.

7 Add cilantro and serve.

VARIATION

To prepare Potato and Peas Kurma, add 1 cup thawed frozen green peas to the above sauce in Step 6.!

Potato and Red Cabbage Stir-fry

[Serves 4]

 This delightful lightly seasoned combination of potatoes and red cabbage is tasty and crunchy. A flavorful and nutritious side dish that is easy to prepare!

1 cup peeled and cubed potatoes (about ½-inch cubes)

1 tablespoon oil

½ teaspoon black mustard seeds

½ teaspoon cumin seeds

¼ teaspoon ground turmeric

¼ teaspoon cayenne pepper powder

½ teaspoon salt more if desired

2 cups shredded red cabbage

¼ teaspoon ground cumin

¼ teaspoon garam masala

1 Steam the potato pieces until they are tender. Set aside.

2 Heat oil in a stainless steel skillet over medium heat. When oil is hot, but not smoking, add black mustard seeds and cumin seeds. Immediately add steamed potatoes, turmeric, cayenne pepper powder, and salt. Gently stir and cook potatoes with the seasonings for about 3 minutes.

3 Add shredded cabbage and stir. Stir in ground cumin, garam masala, and more salt if needed. Cook until cabbage is crisp tender.

Potato Masala

[Serves 4 to 6]

 Seasoned potatoes with tomatoes and ginger can be a wonderful side dish at any meal and a unique, flavorful alternative to plain mashed potatoes. Potato masala is used as a filler in Masala Dosai (page 53) and can also be enjoyed in a veggie wrap.

2 medium Idaho potatoes with skins cut in quarters

½ teaspoon ground turmeric divided

1 teaspoon salt divided

2 tablespoons oil

¼ teaspoon asafoetida powder optional

2 to 4 curry leaves optional

½ teaspoon black mustard seeds

½ teaspoon urad dal

1 cup chopped onions

½ cup chopped tomatoes

1 fresh green chili pepper chopped

1 tablespoon minced fresh ginger

½ teaspoon cayenne pepper powder

¼ cup minced fresh cilantro leaves

1 Cook potatoes with sufficient water to cover with ¼ teaspoon turmeric and ½ teaspoon salt in a covered saucepan over medium heat for approximately 20 minutes or until potatoes become soft. Drain, peel, and coarsely chop potatoes; set aside.

2 In a skillet, heat oil over medium heat. When oil is hot, but not smoking, add asafoetida powder, curry leaves, mustard seeds, and urad dal. Cover and cook until mustard seeds pop and urad dal is golden brown, about 30 seconds.

3 Add onions, tomatoes, green chili pepper, and ginger. Stir-fry for 1 minute. Add the remaining ¼ teaspoon turmeric, remaining ½ teaspoon salt, and the cayenne. Stir well.

4 Add coarsely chopped potatoes and stir gently with ingredients in skillet. Cover and cook over medium heat for 2 to 3 minutes, so flavors will blend well. Taste for seasonings and add more salt, if desired. Add cilantro and mix well.

 Note: A crispy toasted bread sandwich with potato masala filling and a cup of hot tea will hit the spot in the morning or at tea time.

Roasted Potato Medley

[Serves 4 to 6]

 In this dish, yukon gold and sweet potatoes are seasoned with garlic and simple spices. This colorful dish is an excellent accompaniment to any main course.

¾ **pound Yukon Gold potatoes** peeled and cut into cubes (1½ cups)

¾ **pound sweet potatoes** peeled and cut into cubes (1½ cups)

½ **teaspoon ground turmeric**

½ **teaspoon salt** more or less to taste

¼ **teaspoon cayenne pepper powder** more or less to taste

2 **tablespoons oil**

2 **garlic cloves** chopped

¼ **cup chopped green onions**

1 Place cubed potatoes and sweet potatoes in a large glass bowl with ¼ cup of water and cook in microwave on high for 2 minutes; or place in saucepan and boil/steam for 5 minutes on stovetop. They should just be partially cooked and still firm. Drain.

2 Mix together turmeric, salt, and cayenne. Sprinkle on potato mixture and toss until spices are evenly coating them.

3 Heat oil in a skillet over medium-high heat. When the oil is hot but not smoking, add the seasoned potato pieces and garlic to skillet. Cook over medium-low heat for 3 to 5 minutes, stirring to prevent sticking, until potatoes become golden and crisp. (Alternatively, you can spread them on a dark baking sheet and bake at 425°F until crisp.)

4 Sprinkle with green onions, stir and serve.

Roasted Potatoes with Garlic

[Serves 4]

 Lightly seasoned and pan-fried, these crispy potatoes are delicious served as a side dish or with quinoa or flavored rice!

2 cups peeled and cubed Idaho potatoes
   (1-inch cubes)

¼ teaspoon ground turmeric

½ teaspoon salt

½ teaspoon cayenne pepper powder more,
   if desired

½ teaspoon ground cumin

2 tablespoons oil

2 tablespoons chopped garlic cloves

1 Place the cubed potatoes in a glass bowl with ¼ cup water and cook in microwave on high for 2 minutes; or steam potatoes for 3 to 5 minutes on stovetop. Potatoes should still be firm. Drain.

2 Mix together turmeric, salt, cayenne, and cumin. Sprinkle on potatoes and toss until potatoes are evenly coated with spices.

3 Heat oil in a skillet over medium-high heat. When the oil is hot but not smoking, add the seasoned potato pieces and garlic to skillet. Cook over medium-low heat for 3 to 5 minutes, stirring to prevent sticking, until potatoes become golden and crisp. (*Alternatively,* you can spread the potatoes and garlic on a dark baking sheet and bake at 425°F until crisp.)

Red Cabbage and Coconut Stir-fry (Poriyal)

[Serves 4]

 Antioxidant-rich, cruciferous red cabbage makes this stir-fry a crunchy and flavorful side dish!

1 tablespoon oil
1 dried whole red chili pepper
½ teaspoon black mustard seeds
1 teaspoon urad dal
3 cups coarsely shredded red cabbage
1 teaspoon chutney powder*
½ teaspoon salt (more if desired)
1 tablespoon unsweetened shredded coconut

---

*As a substitute for chutney powder, use ½ teaspoon cayenne pepper powder and ½ teaspoon ground cumin

1. Place oil in a stainless steel skillet over medium heat. When oil is hot, but not smoking, stir in dried red chili pepper, mustard seeds, and urad dal. Stir until mustard seeds pop and urad dal is golden brown, about 20 seconds.

2. Add shredded cabbage, chutney powder, and salt. Cook over low heat until cabbage is crisp tender, about 2 to 3 minutes.

3. Add shredded coconut and stir well.

Red Cabbage Raita

 You can make a delicious Red Cabbage Raita using the above cabbage recipe. This raita can be served with any meal for a delicious enhancement.

1 cup cooked Red Cabbage and Coconut Stir-fry cooled
1 to 2 cups plain yogurt or non-dairy substitute
½ teaspoon ground cumin

In a bowl whisk the yogurt and ground cumin together. Add the cooled cabbage mixture and stir.

Tri-Colored Bell Pepper Stir-fry

[Serves 4]

 Crunchy, delicious bell peppers are also rich in Vitamin C. This vibrant, colorful side dish is a perfect way to celebrate summer's bounty of bell peppers.

1 each red, yellow, and green bell peppers

2 teaspoons oil

1 teaspoon black mustard seeds

¼ teaspoon cumin seeds

¼ cup chopped onions

¼ teaspoon cayenne pepper powder

¼ teaspoon ground cumin

½ teaspoon salt

1 Dice bell peppers into 1-inch cubes (about 2 cups mixed); set aside.

2 Heat oil in a skillet over medium heat. When the oil is hot but not smoking, add the mustard seeds and cumin seeds. Stir until mustard seeds pop and cumin seeds turns slightly brown, about 30 seconds.

3 Add onions and stir-fry for 30 seconds. Add the bell peppers, cayenne, ground cumin, and salt. Stir-fry for 3 minutes or until peppers are crisp-tender.

Spinach in Garlic-Lentil Sauce (Spinach Kootu)

[Serves 4 to 6]

 Spinach in a soothing, creamy lentil sauce enhanced with garlic and chili pepper can be served as a side dish at any meal.

1 cup masoor dal (red lentils) or moong dal (yellow lentils)

¼ teaspoon ground turmeric

2 tablespoons oil

1 whole dried red chili pepper

½ teaspoon black mustard seeds

½ teaspoon urad dal

¼ cup chopped onions

4 garlic cloves minced

1 package (10 ounces) frozen chopped spinach thawed*

1 teaspoon ground cumin

1 teaspoon salt

1 fresh green chili pepper chopped (optional)

*You may also use 10 to 12 ounces fresh baby spinach instead of the frozen spinach. Wash, chop, and follow the recipe above to prepare.

1 Bring 4 cups of water to a boil in a deep saucepan. Add dal and turmeric. Reduce heat to medium-high and cook, uncovered, for about 20 to 30 minutes until dal becomes creamy (if water evaporates during the cooking process, add another cup). Set aside.

2 Heat oil in a saucepan over medium heat. When oil is hot, but not smoking, stir in red chili pepper, mustard seeds, and urad dal. Cover and fry until mustard seeds pop and urad dal is golden brown, about 30 seconds.

3 Add onions and garlic and stir-fry for about 1 minute.

4 Stir in thawed spinach, cooked dal, and 1 cup of warm water and stir. Add cumin, salt, and green chili pepper, if desired. Stir well with ingredients in saucepan.

5 Cover and cook over low heat for another 5 to 7 minutes, until spinach is cooked and all flavors are thoroughly blended.

Baby Spinach and Chickpeas with Coconut

[Serves 4]

 This colorful sauté is a delicious, nutritious, and very easy to prepare dish. Protein-packed chickpeas team up with iron-rich spinach in this wholesome combo. It can be enjoyed as a warm salad or as a side dish with any meal.

1 tablespoon oil

¼ teaspoon black mustard seeds

½ teaspoon urad dal

¼ cup chopped onions

2 garlic cloves chopped

1 can (15 ounces) chickpeas (garbanzo beans) rinsed and drained

¼ teaspoon ground turmeric

½ teaspoon chutney powder*

½ teaspoon salt

6 ounces triple-washed baby spinach coarsely chopped

¼ cup fresh shredded coconut or unsweetened shredded coconut

1. Heat oil in a wide non-stick skillet over medium heat. When the oil is hot but not smoking, add mustard seeds and urad dal. Stir until mustard seeds start to pop and urad dal turns golden, about 15 seconds. Immediately add chopped onions and garlic and stir for 1 minute.

2. Add drained chickpeas, turmeric, chutney powder, and salt. Stir for 2 minutes.

3. Add chopped spinach and stir for 1 to 2 minutes. Add coconut and gently stir.

*You can substitute ¼ teaspoon cayenne pepper powder and ¼ teaspoon ground cumin for chutney powder.

Baby Spinach with Yogurt

[Makes 1½ cups]

 This zesty, creamy dish features many immunity boosting ingredients—spinach, garlic, ginger, and yogurt. It can be served as a side dish or as a dip.

1 teaspoon oil

1 teaspoon black mustard seeds

½ teaspoon cumin seeds or urad dal

½ cup chopped onions

¼ of a fresh green chili minced (more or less to taste)

1 tablespoon minced garlic cloves

1 tablespoon grated fresh ginger

4 cups baby spinach chopped

1 teaspoon ground cumin

¼ teaspoon salt more or less to taste

1 tablespoon grated fresh coconut or unsweetened shredded coconut

¾ cup plain low-fat yogurt

1 Heat oil in a skillet over medium-high heat. When the oil is hot but not smoking, add mustard seeds and cumin seeds or urad dal and stir until mustard seeds start to pop and cumin seeds change color from light brown to semi-dark brown, about 30 seconds.

2 Add onions, green chili, garlic, and ginger and cook for 1 to 2 minutes while stirring.

3 Add spinach, ground cumin, and salt. Mix well and cook until spinach is slightly wilted. Add coconut and mix well. *You can serve it as a side vegetable at this point also if you do not want to add yogurt.*

4 Place the cooked spinach in a bowl and allow it to cool. Whisk the yogurt in a separate bowl and stir it into the cool spinach and serve.

Baby Kale in Garlic-Lentil Sauce (Kale Kootu)

[Serves 4]

 Tender baby kale is easy to handle and cook. It is often found boxed in the salad section of grocery stores. Kale is a nutritional powerhouse, especially when combined with lentils and garlic. This is a great side dish with any meal.

½ cup yellow lentils (moong dal)

¼ teaspoon ground turmeric

2 tablespoons oil

½ teaspoon black mustard seeds

½ teaspoon urad dal

½ cup chopped onions

2 to 4 garlic cloves chopped

3 cups baby kale finely chopped

½ teaspoon ground cumin

½ teaspoon salt

1 Rinse moong dal in water twice. Bring 2 cups of water to a boil in a saucepan. Add moong dal and turmeric. Cook uncovered over medium heat until dal becomes soft, about 15 to 20 minutes. (If water evaporates before dal becomes soft, add an additional ½ cup water). Do not drain. Set aside.

2 Heat oil in a saucepan over medium heat. When the oil is hot but not smoking, add mustard seeds and urad dal. Stir until mustard seeds pop and urad dal turns golden, about 20 seconds.

3 Add onions and chopped garlic and stir for 1 minute. Add chopped kale. Stir and cook over medium heat for about 2 minutes.

4 Add reserved and undrained cooked dal to kale mixture. Add ground cumin and salt. If the mixture is thick, add up to an additional ½ cup of warm water. Stir and cook for about 5 minutes over medium heat.

Seasoned Okra and Potato Stir-fry

[Serves 4]

 This lightly seasoned, pan-fried combination of fresh okra with potatoes is a tasty accompaniment to any meal. A delightful side!

3 tablespoons oil

½ teaspoon cumin seeds

1 cup peeled and cubed potato about
   ½-inch cubes

2 to 4 garlic cloves chopped

½ teaspoon ground turmeric

2 cups thinly sliced fresh okra rounds (wash
   and dry okra before cutting)

½ teaspoon cayenne pepper powder

½ teaspoon ground cumin

½ teaspoon salt

1 Heat a non-stick skillet over medium heat. Add 2 tablespoons oil. When oil is hot but not smoking, stir in cumin seeds until light brown, about 20 seconds.

2 Add cubed potatoes, garlic, and turmeric. Stir and cook until potatoes are tender, 3 to 5 minutes.

3 Add sliced okra rounds, cayenne pepper powder, ground cumin, and salt. Stir and coat okra and potatoes with seasonings. Cook over low-medium heat for 2 to 4 minutes.

Summer Squash Medley

[Serves 4]

 Green and yellow zucchini squash, abundant in the summer, will make this a knock out stir-fry!

1 tablespoon oil

1 whole dried red chili pepper

½ teaspoon black mustard seeds

½ teaspoon cumin seeds

1½ cups cubed zucchini

1½ cups cubed yellow squash

¼ teaspoon ground turmeric

½ fresh green chili pepper minced (more or less to taste)

¼ teaspoon salt more or less to taste

2 tablespoons grated fresh coconut or unsweetened dried coconut

1 Heat oil in a skillet over medium-high heat. When the oil is hot but not smoking, add the red chili pepper, mustard seeds, and cumin seeds and stir until mustard seeds start to pop and cumin seeds change color from light brown to semi-dark brown, about 30 seconds.

2 Add zucchini, yellow squash, turmeric, green chili pepper, and salt. Stir-fry over medium-low heat for 2 minutes.

3 Stir in coconut and serve.

Sweet Potato Stir-fry (Poriyal)

[Makes 2 cups]

 This lightly seasoned recipe enhances the natural, hearty flavor of sweet potatoes. Perfect as a side with any meal.

1 pound sweet potatoes peeled and cut into 1-inch cubes (about 2 cups)

1 tablespoon oil

1 whole dried red chili pepper

½ teaspoon black mustard seeds

¼ teaspoon cumin seeds

½ teaspoon cayenne pepper powder

¼ teaspoon salt

1 tablespoon unsweetened shredded coconut

1 Steam sweet potatoes in a saucepan about 5 minutes until tender. Set aside.

2 Heat oil in a skillet over medium heat. When the oil is hot but not smoking, add the red chili pepper, mustard seeds, and cumin seeds. Stir until mustard seeds start to pop and cumin seeds change color to light brown, about 30 seconds.

3 Add steamed sweet potatoes, cayenne pepper powder, and salt. Gently mix with the seasonings for a minute. Add coconut and gently mix. Serve warm.

Sweet Potato, Black Beans and Spinach Wraps

[Serves 4]

 This colorful combination of super foods with seasonings makes a delicious breakfast or lunch wrap. It can also be served as a side dish. Peanut and Coconut Chutney (page 37) is an excellent accompaniment to these wraps.

2 small sweet potatoes peeled and cubed

2 tablespoons oil

½ teaspoon cumin seeds

½ cup chopped onions

3 cloves garlic finely chopped

½ of a 15-ounce can low-sodium black beans rinsed and drained

1 cup chopped baby spinach

½ teaspoon cayenne pepper powder

½ teaspoon ground cumin

¼ teaspoon salt

4 medium flour or wheat tortillas or gluten free wraps

1 Steam the sweet potatoes for 5 minutes. Set aside. (You can also microwave the sweet potatoes on high until tender and then cube.)

2 Heat oil in a skillet. When oil is warm, add cumin seeds and let it slightly brown, about 15 seconds.

3 Add onions and garlic and saute for 1 minute. Add steamed sweet potatoes, black beans, and chopped spinach. Stir gently and cook for about 2 minutes.

4 Add cayenne pepper powder, ground cumin, and salt. Stir gently.

To make a wrap: Lightly brush both sides of a tortilla with oil and warm it in a skillet, flipping once. Remove tortilla to a plate. Place some of the vegetable mixture in the tortilla, fold and make a wrap.

Swiss Chard Lentil Crumble

[Serves 6]

 A unique and innovative colorful swiss chard dish enhanced with crumbled yellow split peas and seasonings. A powerful combination of nutrition and flavor!

⅓ cup yellow split peas

1 whole dried red chili pepper more or less to taste

½ teaspoon fennel seeds

1½ teaspoons cumin seeds divided

3 tablespoons oil

½ teaspoon black mustard seeds

1 cup chopped onions

½ teaspoon ground turmeric

½ teaspoon cayenne pepper powder more or less to taste

¼ teaspoon salt more or less to taste

4 cups chopped Swiss chard including stems

3 tablespoons grated fresh coconut or unsweetened dried coconut

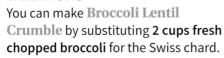

VARIATIONS

You can make **Broccoli Lentil Crumble** by substituting **2 cups fresh chopped broccoli** for the Swiss chard.

Or try **Green Beans Lentil Crumble** by substituting **2 cups chopped green beans** for the Swiss chard.

1 Place split peas in a bowl and add enough hot water to cover. Let soak for 30 minutes. Drain.

2 Place soaked and drained peas in a blender or food processor with red chili pepper, fennel seeds, cumin seeds, and ¼ cup of warm water. Blend or process until the texture of coarse cornmeal. Pour mixture in a microwave-safe dish, cover with paper towel, and cook on high for 3 minutes—mixture will feel somewhat firm. Cool for 5 minutes; break into small pieces with a fork; reserve crumble.

3 Heat oil in a skillet over medium-high heat. When the oil is hot but not smoking, add mustard seeds and cumin seeds and stir until mustard seeds start to pop and cumin seeds change color from light brown to semi-dark brown, about 30 seconds. Add onions and stir-fry for 30 seconds.

4 Add reserved split pea crumble, turmeric, cayenne, and salt. Stir well. Continue to stir while cooking over medium-low heat for 3 to 5 minutes, until the split peas become golden and grainy in texture.

5 Stir in Swiss chard, cover, and cook over low heat 3 to 5 minutes until chard becomes tender, stirring frequently.

6 Add coconut, stir, and serve.

Vibrant Vegetables in Almond-Coconut Sauce (Vegetable Kurma)

[Serves 6]

 Vegetable Kurma is a true specialty in Indian cooking. A colorful blend of vegetables is cooked in a delicately spiced yet rich almond-coconut sauce. It can be enjoyed with rice or quinoa or with flatbreads like naan.

2 cups peeled and cubed Idaho potato (1 inch)

1 tablespoon unsalted butter

1 tablespoon oil

2 to 4 curry leaves optional

1 bay leaf

3 or 4 (½-inch-long) slivers cinnamon sticks

¼ teaspoon cumin seeds

¼ teaspoon fennel seeds

1 cup chopped onions

1 cup chopped tomatoes divided

1½ cups cauliflower florets

½ teaspoon ground turmeric

1 teaspoon curry powder

½ teaspoon salt more if desired

1 cup frozen peas and carrots thawed

Spice Paste

½ cup unsweetened shredded coconut

1 fresh green chili pepper more if desired

14 raw almonds

1 tablespoon white poppy seeds optional

1 teaspoon cumin seeds

1 teaspoon fennel seeds

2 thick slices fresh ginger

1 Place all the ingredients for the spice paste in a blender. Add 2 cups of hot water and grind the ingredients to a smooth paste. Set aside.

2 Par-boil the cubed potatoes: in a bowl place cubed potatoes with one tablespoon water and microwave on high for 2 to 3 minutes. Set aside.

3 Heat butter and oil in a wide-bottomed saucepan over medium heat. When oil is hot but not smoking, add curry leaves, bay leaf, cinnamon sticks, cumin seeds, and fennel seeds. Cover and fry to a golden brown, about 30 seconds.

4 Add onions and ½ cup of the chopped tomatoes and stir-fry for 1 minute until onions are lightly translucent.

5 Add par-boiled potatoes, cauliflower florets, and turmeric and stir well. Add curry powder and salt and stir-fry for 1 to 2 minutes. Add spice paste from blender and 2 cups of hot water. Stir the mixture and cook for 2 to 3 minutes.

6 Add thawed carrots and peas and 1 cup of warm water and cook for 2 minutes. Add the remaining ½ cup tomatoes and gently stir. Cover and cook for a couple of minutes until the flavors are blended together.

7 Add another ½ cup warm water (or coconut cream) if needed to get desired consistency. Stir and serve.

Vegetable Medley in a Hurry

[Serves 4]

Carrots, green peas, corn, black beans, and green beans are all good sources of fiber. In this recipe, we use a package of frozen mixed vegetables so this delicious side dish comes together in just a few minutes!

1 tablespoon oil

1 whole dried red chili pepper

½ teaspoon black mustard seeds*

½ teaspoon urad dal*

1 package (16 ounces) frozen mixed
   vegetables thawed

1 teaspoon chutney powder**

½ teaspoon salt

---

*As a substitute for mustard seeds and urad dal, you can use 1 teaspoon of cumin seeds.

**As a substitute for chutney powder you can use ½ teaspoon cayenne pepper and ½teaspoon ground cumin.

1 Heat oil in a skillet over medium heat. When oil is hot but not smoking, add red chili pepper, mustard seeds, and urad dal. Stir until mustard seeds pop and urad dal turns golden, about 20 seconds.

2 Stir in thawed vegetables and mix with the seasonings.

3 Add chutney powder and salt. Stir and cook over medium heat for about 2 to 3 minutes.

Zucchini Dal

[Serves 4]

Mildly seasoned zucchini cooked in lentil sauce! This delicious, soothing side dish is a perfect comfort food and can be enjoyed with rice, quinoa, or naan.

¾ cup yellow lentils (moong dal)

½ teaspoon ground turmeric divided

2 tablespoons oil

1 whole dried red chili pepper

½ teaspoon cumin seeds

½ cup chopped onions

2 cups peeled and diced zucchini (about ½-inch cubes)

¼ teaspoon cayenne pepper powder

1 teaspoon ground cumin

1 teaspoon salt

2 tablespoons shredded ginger

¼ cup chopped cilantro

VARIATION

You can create a delightful **Eggplant Dal** by substituting diced eggplant for the zucchini in the above recipe.

1 Bring 3 cups of water to a boil in a tall saucepan over medium heat. Add moong dal and ¼ teaspoon ground turmeric. Reduce heat to medium and cook, uncovered, for about 30 minutes until dal becomes creamy. If water evaporates during the cooking process, add up to another cup of water. Set aside.

2 Place oil in a saucepan over medium heat. When oil is hot, but not smoking, add whole dried red chili pepper and cumin seeds and cook for about 20 seconds.

3 Add onions and stir for 1 minute. Add zucchini and the remaining ¼ teaspoon turmeric. Stir well into seasonings in saucepan.

4 Add cayenne pepper powder, ground cumin, and salt. Stir well. Add creamy moong dal and 1 cup of warm water. Stir.

5 Add ginger and cook, covered, over medium heat until zucchini becomes tender, about 5 to 7 minutes, stirring occasionally. Garnish with chopped cilantro.

Desserts

Fruit and Yogurt Medley

[Makes 2½ cups]

 Yogurt "desserts," typically laden with fruit, nuts, and spices, are common in India. This dish tastes like a creamy treat, but is still packed with a variety of appealing fruits.

1½ cups plain low-fat yogurt

½ teaspoon sugar or stevia equivalent

½ teaspoon ground cumin

⅛ teaspoon cayenne pepper powder

½ cup halved seedless black or red grapes

½ cup halved seedless green grapes

½ firm banana sliced

1 (5-ounce) can mandarin oranges drained

¼ cup chopped walnuts

1 Whisk the yogurt, sugar or stevia, cumin, and cayenne in a bowl until smooth.

2 Reserve a few pieces of each fruit and the walnuts for garnish. Add remaining grapes, banana, oranges, and walnuts to yogurt mixture and stir gently.

3 Serve garnished with reserved fruit and nuts.

Mango Lassi

[Serves 4]

 Serve this lassi chilled as a refreshing hot weather drink.

1 can (about 30 ounce) **mango pulp**

30 ounces **low-fat cultured buttermilk** or **unsweetened vanilla almond milk**

Sugar or **honey** as desired

2 tablespoons **rose essence*** optional

Rum to taste optional

---

*Rose essence is used throughout India and the Middle East for sweets. You should be able to find it at Indian or Middle Eastern grocers.

1 Put all the ingredients except rum in a large punch bowl. Whisk until well blended. Adjust level of sweetness. Refrigerate and serve cold.

2 To serve, pour over crushed ice in a tall glass. If using rum add 2 tablespoons rum to each glass.

Tapioca Payasam

[Serves 4]

 This irresistible, creamy tapioca dessert is flavored with saffron and cardamom.

¼ cup raw cashew halves

1 tablespoon unsalted butter divided

½ cup tapioca (not quick-cooking)

3 cups 2-percent or whole milk

¼ teaspoon ground cardamom

4 to 6 saffron threads

2 very small pieces cystalline camphor
   optional

½ cup sugar more, if desired

¼ cup raisins optional

1 Fry cashew halves in ½ tablespoon butter in a small skillet or butter warmer over medium heat until evenly cooked. Remove cashews from skillet and set aside.

2 Melt the remaining ½ tablespoon butter in a deep saucepan. Add tapioca and cook for a few minutes, stirring constantly.

3 Slowly add milk in 1 cup increments, stirring all the while over medium to low heat, until tapioca cooks, about 15 minutes. When tapioca is cooked it will increase in size and will become softer.

4 Add cardamom, saffron threads, crystalline camphor, if using, and sugar. Stir well over low heat. Add cashew halves and raisins, if desired.

5 You may serve payasam at room temperature or as a cold dessert.

If room temperature is preferred: remove payasam from heat, cover and leave at room temperature until time of serving. Add additional warm milk and sugar as desired before serving.

If you prefer to serve payasam cold: put in the refrigerator, where it will thicken. Before serving, place it in a microwave oven and warm for a minute or two. Stir well and add additional cold milk until payasam reaches your desired consistency. You may also add additional sugar as desired.

Sweet Black Rice with Cardamom and Coconut

[Serves 4]

 A delectable dessert made with whole-grain black rice that's slightly sweet and sticky with a hint of spice.

1 cup black rice

1 cup sugar

½ teaspoon ground cardamom

2 tablespoons melted unsalted butter (ghee)

½ cup grated fresh coconut or sweetened shredded coconut

1 Bring 3 cups of water to a boil and then add rice. Cook rice about 25 minutes or until soft. (A rice cooker or pressure cooker can be used to cook rice quickly.)

2 Put cooked rice in a bowl and add sugar, cardamom, melted butter, and coconut. Mix well.

3 Serve at room temperature or cold, and garnish with fruit as desired.

Index

var. = variation

ADAIS
  Multigrain Savory Crepes (Adais), 49
ALMONDS
  Potato and Peas Kurma, 191 (*var.*)
  Potato in Almond Coconut Sauce (Potato
    Kurma), 191
  Vibrant Vegetables in Almond Coconut Sauce
    (Vegetable Kurma), 223
APPETIZERS
  Black Bean Cutlets, 19
  Creamy Apple Chutney Dip, 36 (*var.*)
  Potato Cutlets, 21
  Roasted Vegetable Kebabs, 23
APPLES
  Chickpea and Apple Rice, 73
  Chickpeas with Ginger and Apple, 137 (*var.*)
  Creamy Apple Chutney Dip, 36 (*var.*)
  Seasoned Apple Relish, 36
ASPARAGUS
  Asparagus with Shallots and Garlic, 117
  Tender Asparagus with Ginger and Coconut, 119
  Tofu Scrambler with Asparagus and Carrots, 55

BEANS, BLACK
  Black Bean Cutlets, 19
  Sweet Potato, Black Beans and Spinach Wraps,
    219
BEANS, GREEN
  Carrot and Green Beans Sambhar, 101 (var.)
  Five-Color Vegetable Blend with Lentils, 139
  Green Beans in Lentil Sauce (Kootu), 165
  Green Beans Lentil Crumble, 221 (*var.*)
  Green Beans and Yellow Lentil Stir-fry (Poriyal),
    171
  Green Beans Sambhar, 103
  Vibrant Green Beans with Carrot Stir-fry
    (Poriyal), 169
  Seasoned Green Beans with Coconut, 167

Sweet Potato Quinoa Soup, 45
BEANS, WHITE (CANNELLINI, NAVY)
  Cannellini Beans with Broccoli, 129
  Sweet Potato Quinoa Soup, 45
BEETS
  Beet and Lentil Soup, 43 (*var.*)
  Beet Fritters (Beet Vadais), 24 (*var.*)
  Stir-fried Beets with Coconut, 123
BELL PEPPERS
  Bell Pepper and Radish Sambhar, 95
  Bell Pepper and Tomato Rice with Cashews, 65
  Multicolored Bell Peppers in Lentil Sauce, 125
  Tri-Colored Pepper Stir-fry, 203
BIRIYANI
  Vegetable Biriyani, 87
BLACK-EYED PEAS
  Black-eyed Peas Kulambu, 107
  Black-eyed Peas Masala, 127
BREADS
  Pooris, 59
BREAKFAST DISHES
  Dosais, 52
  Cracked Wheat Uppuma, 51 (*var.*)
  Cream of Wheat Uppuma, 51
  Masala Dosais, 53 (*var.*)
  Multigrain Savory Crepes (Adais), 49
  Onion Dosais, 53 (*var.*)
  Pooris, 59
  Quinoa Uppuma, 51 (*var.*)
  Tofu Scrambler with Asparagus and Carrots, 55
  Uthappams, 57
  Vegetable Uppuma, 51 (*var.*)
  Wheat-based Buttermilk Plain Dosais, 53 (*var.*)
BROCCOLI
  Broccoli Lentil Crumble, 221 (*var.*)
  Broccoli with Coconut Stir-fry (Poriyal), 128
  Cannellini Beans with Broccoli, 129

BRUSSELS SPROUTS
  Brussels Sprouts Kulambu, 97
  Brussels Sprouts Masala, 133
  Brussels Sprouts with Chickpeas (Poriyal), 131

CABBAGE
  Cabbage and Carrot Kootu, 143 (*var.*)
  Cabbage and Green Peas Stir-fry, 145 (*var.*)
  Cabbage, Carrot and Farro Salad, 145 (*var.*)
  Cabbage in Lentil Sauce (Kootu), 143
  Cabbage with Carrots Stir-fry (Poriyal), 145
  Five-Color Vegetable Blend with Lentils, 139
  Plain Cabbage Stir-fry, 145 (*var.*)
  Potato and Red Cabbage Stir-fry, 193
  Red Cabbage and Coconut Stir-fry (Poriyal), 201
  Red Cabbage Raita, 201

CARROTS
  Cabbage and Carrot Kootu, 143 (*var.*)
  Cabbage, Carrot and Farro Salad, 145 (*var.*)
  Cabbage with Carrots Stir-fry (Poriyal), 145
  Carrot and Green Beans Sambhar, 101 (*var.*)
  Carrot and Lentil Soup with Kale, 41
  Carrot and Peas Rice with Cashews, 69 (*var.*)
  Carrot Sambhar, 101
  Five-Color Vegetable Blend with Lentils, 139
  Seasoned Carrots with Coconut (Poriyal), 147
  Tofu Scrambler with Asparagus and Carrots, 55
  Vegetable Biriyani, 87
  Vibrant Carrot Rice Pilaf, 69
  Vibrant Green Beans with Carrot Stir-fry
    (Poriyal), 169

CASHEWS
  Bell Pepper and Tomato Rice with Cashews, 65
  Black Pepper and Cumin Rice, 67
  Carrot and Peas Rice with Cashews, 69 (*var.*)
  Coconut Rice, 75
  Hearty Cauliflower Rice, 71
  Mushroom and Green Peas Cashew Kurma, 181 (*var.*)
  Mushroom Cashew Kurma, 181
  Spinach Lentil Rice, 81
  Tapioca Payasam, 233
  Tomato Rice with Green Onions, 83
  Vibrant Carrot Rice Pilaf, 69

CAULIFLOWER
  Aloo Gobi, 149
  Cauliflower, Potato and Green Peas Medley, 155
  Cauliflower and Lentil Soup, 43
  Cauliflower in Lentil Sauce (Kootu), 151
  Cauliflower Masala, 153
  Hearty Cauliflower Rice, 71
  Vegetable Biriyani, 87
  Vibrant Vegetables in Almond Coconut Sauce
    (Vegetable Kurma), 223

CHICKPEAS (GARBANZO BEANS)
  Baby Spinach and Chickpeas with Coconut, 207
  Brussels Sprouts with Chickpeas (Poriyal), 131
  Chana Masala, 157
  Chickpea and Apple Rice, 73
  Chickpeas with Ginger and Apple, 137 (*var.*)
  Chickpeas with Ginger and Mango, 137
  Sweet Potato Quinoa Soup, 45

CHILI PEPPERS
  about, 13, 14

CHUTNEYS/RELISHES. *See also* RAITAS
  Cilantro Chutney, 33
  Eggplant Chutney, 31
  Peanut and Coconut Chutney, 37
  Seasoned Apple Relish, 36
  Tomato and Onion Chutney, 39

CILANTRO
  Cilantro Chutney, 33

COCONUT
  about, 12
  Baby Spinach and Chickpeas with Coconut, 207
  Coconut Rice, 75
  Lentil Crumble with Coconut, 173
  Lima Beans and Coconut Stir-fry, 179
  Peanut and Coconut Chutney, 37
  Red Cabbage and Coconut Stir-fry (Poriyal), 201
  Red Cabbage Raita, 201
  Sautéed Baby Kale with Lentils and Coconut
    (Kale Poriyal), 121
  Sautéed Baby Spinach with Lentils and Coconut
    (Spinach Poriyal), 121 (*var.*)
  Savory Rice Lentil Balls (Kolakkatai), 27
  Seasoned Green Beans with Coconut, 167

Stir-fried Beets with Coconut, 123
Sweet Black Rice with Cardamom and Coconut, 26
CORN
  Sweet Potato Quinoa Soup, 45
CREPES/PANCAKES
  Dosais, 52
  Masala Dosais, 53 (*var.*)
  Multigrain Savory Crepes (Adais), 49
  Onion Dosais, 53 (*var.*)
  Uthappams, 57
  Wheat-based Buttermilk Plain Dosais, 53 (*var.*)
CUTLETS/PATTIES
  Black Bean Cutlets, 19
  Potato Cutlets, 21

DALS/LEGUMES/LENTILS. *See also* CHICKPEAS; BLACK-EYED PEAS
  about, 7, 11, 93
  Baby Kale in Garlic-Lentil Sauce (Kale Kootu), 211
  Beet and Lentil Soup, 43 (*var.*)
  Beet Fritters (Beet Vadais), 24 (*var.*)
  Bell Pepper and Radish Sambhar, 95
  Broccoli Lentil Crumble, 221 (*var.*)
  Brussels Sprouts Kulambu, 97
  Carrot and Lentil Soup with Kale, 41
  Carrot Sambhar, 101
  Cauliflower and Lentil Soup, 43
  Cauliflower in Lentil Sauce (Kootu), 151
  Eggplant Dal, 227 (*var.*)
  Eggplant in Lentil Sauce, 165 (*var.*)
  Five-Color Vegetable Blend with Lentils, 139
  Green Beans and Yellow Lentil Stir-fry (Poriyal), 171
  Green Beans Lentil Crumble, 221 (*var.*)
  Green Beans Sambhar, 103
  Kohlrabi Sambhar, 105
  Lentil Crumble with Coconut, 173
  Lentil Fritters (Masala Vadai), 25
  Multicolored Bell Peppers in Lentil Sauce, 125
  Multigrain Savory Crepes (Adais), 49
  Okra Sambhar, 109

Pearl Onion and Tomato Sambhar, 111
Potatoes in Lentil Sauce, 189
Sautéed Baby Kale with Lentils and Coconut (Kale Poriyal), 121
Sautéed Baby Spinach with Lentils and Coconut (Spinach Poriyal), 121 (*var.*)
Savory Rice Lentil Balls (Kolakkatai), 27
Spinach Fritters (Spinach Vadais), 24 (*var.*)
Spinach in Garlic Lentil Sauce (Spinach Kootu), 205
Spinach Lentil Rice, 81
Swiss Chard Lentil Crumble, 221
Tomato and Lentil Soup, 43 (*var.*)
Zucchini Dal, 227
DESSERTS
  Creamy Yogurt Rice, 85
  Fruit and Yogurt Medley, 230
  Mango Lassi, 231
  Sweet Black Rice with Cardamom and Coconut, 234
  Tapioca Payasam, 233
DIPS
  Creamy Apple Chutney Dip, 36 (*var.*)
  Peanut and Coconut Chutney, 37
DOSAIS
  Dosais, 52
  Masala Dosais, 53 (*var.*)
  Onion Dosais, 53 (*var.*)
  Uthappams, 57
  Wheat-based Buttermilk Dosais, 53 (*var.*)

EGGPLANT
  Eggplant and Potato Masala, 161
  Eggplant Chutney, 31
  Eggplant Dal, 227 (*var.*)
  Eggplant in Lentil Sauce, 165 (*var.*)
  Eggplant in Seasoned Tamarind Sauce (Kosamalli), 35
  Eggplant Kootu, 165 (*var.*)
  Indian Ratatouille, 163
  Seasoned Baby Eggplant Stir-fry, 159

FARRO
  Cabbage, Carrot and Farro Salad, 145 (*var.*)
FRITTERS. *See* PATTIES/CUTLETS/FRITTERS
FRUITS. *See also* APPLES; CRANBERRIES;
    MANGOES; POMEGRANATE
  Fruit and Yogurt Medley, 230

GREEN BEANS. *See* BEANS, GREEN
GREEN PEAS. *See* PEAS, GREEN
GREENS. *See* KALE; SPINACH; SWISS CHARD

KALE
  Baby Kale in Garlic-Lentil Sauce (Kale Kootu),
    211
  Carrot and Lentil Soup with Kale, 41
  Sautéed Baby Kale with Lentils and Coconut
    (Kale Poriyal), 121
KEBABS
  Roasted Vegetable Kebabs, 23
KOHLRABI
  Kohlrabi Sambhar, 105
KOOTUS
  Baby Kale in Garlic-Lentil Sauce (Kale Kootu),
    211
  Cabbage and Carrot Kootu, 143 (*var.*)
  Cabbage in Lentil Sauce (Kootu), 143
  Cauliflower in Lentil Sauce (Kootu), 151
  Eggplant Kootu, 165 (*var.*)
  Green Beans in Lentil Sauce (Kootu), 165
  Spinach in Garlic Lentil Sauce (Spinach Kootu),
    205
  Zucchini Kootu, 165 (*var.*)
KULAMBUS
  about 93
  Black-eyed Peas Kulambu, 107
  Brussels Sprouts Kulambu, 97
KURMAS
  Mushroom and Green Peas Cashew Kurma, 181 (*var.*)
  Mushroom Cashew Kurma, 181
  Potato and Peas Kurma, 191 (*var.*)
  Potato in Almond Coconut Sauce (Potato
    Kurma), 191
  Vibrant Vegetables in Almond Coconut Sauce
    (Vegetable Kurma), 223

LASSIS (DRINKS)
  Mango Lassi, 231
LEGUMES. *See* DALS/LEGUMES/LENTILS
LEMON
  Fragrant Lemon Rice, 77
LENTILS. *See* DALS/LEGUMES/LENTILS
LIMA BEANS
  Heavenly Lima Beans Masala, 177
  Lima Beans and Coconut Stir-fry, 179

MANGOES
  Chickpeas with Ginger and Mango, 137
  Black-eyed Peas Kulambu, 107
  Mango Lassi, 231
MUSHROOMS
  Mushroom and Green Peas Cashew Kurma,
    181 (*var.*)
  Mushroom Cashew Kurma, 181
  Mushroom Masala, 183
  Savory Mushroom Rice, 79

NUTS. *See* ALMONDS; CASHEWS; PEANUTS

ONIONS
  Onion Tomato Raita, 84
  Tomato and Onion Raita, 39 (*var.*)
  Pearl Onion and Tomato Sambhar, 111
OKRA
  Okra Masala (Bhindi Masala), 185
  Okra Sambhar, 109
  Seasoned Okra and Potato Stir-fry, 213

PANCAKES. *See* CREPES/PANCAKES; RICE CAKES/
    PANCAKES
PANEER
  Matar Paneer, 175
PARSNIPS
  Parsnips with Green Peas, 187
PATTIES/CUTLETS/FRITTERS
  Beet Fritters (Beet Vadais), 24 (*var.*)
  Black Bean Cutlets, 19
  Lentil Fritters (Masala Vadais), 25
  Potato Cutlets, 21
  Spinach Fritters (Spinach Vadais), 24 (*var.*)

PAYASAMS
  Tapioca Payasam, 233
PEANUTS
  Peanut and Coconut Chutney, 37
PEAS, GREEN
  Cabbage and Green Peas Stir-fry, 145 (*var.*)
  Cauliflower, Potato and Green Peas Medley, 155
  Matar Paneer, 175
  Matar Tofu, 175 (*var.*)
  Mushroom and Green Peas Cashew Kurma,
    181 (*var.*)
  Parsnips with Green Peas, 187
  Potato and Peas Kurma, 191 (*var.*)
  Vegetable Biriyani, 87
PEPPERS. *See* BELL PEPPERS; CHILI PEPPERS
POORIS
  Pooris, 59
PORIYALS
  Broccoli with Coconut Stir-fry (Poriyal), 128
  Brussels Sprouts with Chickpeas (Poriyal), 131
  Cabbage with Carrots Stir-fry (Poriyal), 145
  Green Beans and Yellow Lentil Stir-fry (Poriyal),
    171
  Red Cabbage and Coconut Stir-fry (Poriyal), 201
  Sautéed Baby Kale with Lentils and Coconut
    (Kale Poriyal), 121
  Seasoned Carrots with Coconut (Poriyal), 147
  Sweet Potato Stir-fry (Poriyal), 217
  Vibrant Green Beans with Carrot Stir-fry
    (Poriyal), 169
POTATOES
  Aloo Gobi, 149
  Cauliflower, Potato and Green Peas Medley, 155
  Eggplant and Potato Masala, 161
  Masala Dosais, 53 (*var.*)
  Potato and Peas Kurma, 191 (*var.*)
  Potato and Red Cabbage Stir-fry, 193
  Potato Cutlets, 21
  Potato in Almond Coconut Sauce (Potato
    Kurma), 191
  Potato Masala, 195
  Potatoes in Lentil Sauce, 189
  Roasted Potato Medley, 197

  Roasted Potatoes with Garlic, 199
  Seasoned Okra and Potato Stir-fry, 213
  Vegetable Biriyani, 87
  Vibrant Vegetables in Almond Coconut Sauce
    (Vegetable Kurma), 223

QUINOA
  about, 10, 63
  Colorful Vegetable Quinoa, 89
  Quinoa Uppuma, 51 (*var.*)
  Sweet Potato Quinoa Soup, 45

RADISHES
  Bell Pepper and Radish Sambhar, 95
RAITAS
  Onion Tomato Raita, 84
  Red Cabbage Raita, 201
  Tomato and Onion Raita, 39 (*var.*)
RICE. *See also* RICE CAKES/PANCAKES
  about, 10, 63
  Bell Pepper and Tomato Rice with Cashews, 65
  Black Pepper and Cumin Rice, 67
  Carrot and Peas Rice with Cashews, 69 (*var.*)
  Chickpea and Apple Rice, 73
  Coconut Rice, 75
  Creamy Yogurt Rice, 85
  Fragrant Lemon Rice, 77
  Hearty Cauliflower Rice, 71
  Savory Mushroom Rice, 79
  Savory Rice Lentil Balls (Kolakkatai), 27
  Savory Yogurt Rice, 85 (*var.*)
  Spinach Lentil Rice, 81
  Sweet Black Rice with Cardamom and Coconut,
    234
  Tomato Rice with Green Onions, 83
  Vegetable Biriyani, 87
  Vibrant Carrot Rice Pilaf, 69
RICE CAKES/PANCAKES
  Dosais, 52
  Masala Dosais, 53 (*var.*)
  Onion Dosais, 53 (*var.*)
  Uthappams, 57
  Wheat-based Buttermilk Plain Dosais, 53 (*var.*)

SAMBHARS
  about, 93
  Bell Pepper and Radish Sambhar, 95
  Carrot and Green Beans Sambhar, 101 (*var.*)
  Carrot Sambhar, 101
  Green Beans Sambhar, 103
  Kohlrabi Sambhar, 105
  Okra Sambhar, 109
  Pearl Onion and Tomato Sambhar, 111
  Zucchini Sambhar, 113
SHALLOTS
  Asparagus with Shallots and Garlic, 117
SOUPS
  Beet and Lentil Soup, 43 (*var.*)
  Black-eyed Peas Kulambu, 107
  Carrot and Lentil Soup with Kale, 41
  Cauliflower and Lentil Soup, 43
  Sweet Potato Quinoa Soup, 45
  Tomato and Lentil Soup, 43 (*var.*)
SPINACH
  Baby Spinach and Chickpeas with Coconut, 207
  Baby Spinach with Yogurt, 209
  Sautéed Baby Spinach with Lentils and Coconut (Spinach Poriyal), 121 (*var.*)
  Spinach Fritters (Spinach Vadais), 24 (*var.*)
  Spinach in Garlic Lentil Sauce (Spinach Kootu), 205
  Spinach Lentil Rice, 81
  Sweet Potato, Black Beans and Spinach Wraps, 219
SPLIT PEAS. *See* DALS/LEGUMES/LENTILS
SQUASH (BUTTERNUT, SPAGHETTI, SUMMER, YELLOW). *See also* ZUCCHINI
  Butternut Squash in Tamarind Sauce, 99
  Cumin-Scented Butternut Squash, 135
  Spiced Spaghetti Squash, 141
  Summer Squash Medley, 215
SWEET POTATOES
  Roasted Potato Medley, 197
  Sweet Potato, Black Beans and Spinach Wraps, 219
  Sweet Potato Stir-fry (Poriyal), 217
  Sweet Potato Quinoa Soup, 45

SWISS CHARD
  Swiss Chard Lentil Crumble, 221

TOFU
  Matar Tofu, 175 (*var.*)
  Tofu Scrambler with Asparagus and Carrots, 55
TOMATOES
  Bell Pepper and Tomato Rice with Cashews, 65
  Indian Ratatouille, 163
  Multicolored Bell Peppers in Lentil Sauce, 125
  Onion Tomato Raita, 84
  Pearl Onion and Tomato Sambhar, 111
  Potatoes in Lentil Sauce, 189
  Tomato and Onion Chutney, 39
  Tomato and Onion Raita, 39 (*var.*)
  Potato and Peas Kurma, 191 (*var.*)
  Potato in Almond Coconut Sauce (Potato Kurma), 191
  Tomato and Lentil Soup, 43 (*var.*)
  Tomato Rice with Green Onions, 83

UPPUMAS
  Cracked Wheat Uppuma, 51 (*var.*)
  Cream of Wheat Uppuma, 51
  Quinoa Uppuma, 51 (*var.*)
  Vegetable Uppuma, 51 (*var.*)

VEGETABLES. *See also* ASPARAGUS; BEANS, GREEN; BEETS; BELL PEPPERS; BROCCOLI; BRUSSELS SPROUTS; CABBAGE; CARROTS; CAULIFLOWER; CORN; CUCUMBERS; EGGPLANTS; KALE; KOHLRABI; LIMA BEANS; MUSHROOMS; OKRA; PARSNIPS; PEAS, GREEN; RADISHES; SPINACH; TOMATOES
  Colorful Vegetable Quinoa, 89
  Five-Color Vegetable Blend with Lentils, 139
  Roasted Vegetable Kebabs, 23
  Vibrant Vegetables in Almond Coconut Sauce (Vegetable Kurma), 223
  Vegetable Biriyani, 87
  Vegetable Medley in a Hurry, 225
  Vegetable Uppuma, 51 (var.)

WHEAT (CREAM OF; CRACKED; GRAHAM)
Cracked Wheat Uppuma, 51 (*var.*)
Cream of Wheat Uppuma, 51
Pooris, 59
Vegetable Uppuma, 51 (*var.*)

YOGURT
Baby Spinach with Yogurt, 209
Cilantro Chutney, 33
Creamy Apple Chutney Dip, 36 (*var.*)
Creamy Yogurt Rice, 85
Fruit and Yogurt Medley, 230
Onion Tomato Raita, 84
Savory Yogurt Rice, 85 (*var.*)
Tomato and Onion Raita, 39 (*var.*)

ZUCCHINI
Indian Ratatouille, 163
Summer Squash Medley, 215
Zucchini Dal, 227
Zucchini Kootu, 165 (*var.*)
Zucchini Sambhar, 113

ACKNOWLEDGMENTS

The motivation and encouragement to write this book came from many sources, including my family, Hippocrene publisher Priti Gress, and importantly from many viewers of my TV shows and users of my earlier books. It has been my great pleasure to work with Priti, the editor for all my books published by Hippocrene Books. I could not have hoped for a better and more supportive editor. My thanks also to Barbara Keane-Pigeon for her diligent editing and production work on this book.

I also owe gratitude to many people who have encouraged me or made helpful suggestions with this project. I must mention Ashok Vairavan, Valli Vairavan, Dr. Atul Gupta, Muthu Nachiappan, Dr. Kumar Alagappan, Margaret Pfeiffer, Sreedevi Vinnakota, Linda Smallpage (who took all the beautiful photos in the book), Buji Annaprasad, and Dr. Patricia Marquart. Margaret and Muthu even tried many recipes and offered useful suggestions. Both Pat and Margaret also co-authored previous books with me. I also want to thank Gudi Chauhan for helping me research online sites for spices.

I was also energized by my ten-year-old twin grandsons, Surav and Mihir, who regularly checked on my progress with this cookbook.

Finally, I am deeply grateful to my husband Dr. K. Vairavan for his inspiration and unbounded support throughout this book project.

# ABOUT THE AUTHOR

Alamelu Vairavan has a passion for educating people about healthful cooking using spices, vegetables, and legumes. She has authored many cookbooks and hosted the popular television series, "Healthful Indian Flavors with Alamelu," produced by Milwaukee PBS and shown nationally on PBS CREATE. Her shows can also be viewed on YouTube.

Besides her own TV series, Alamelu has appeared as a guest on several national and regional television and radio programs. She has also given numerous public presentations and was a featured author and presenter at the Kohler Food and Wine Experience and at Wisconsin Wine and Dine events. She was a featured chef and author at a sold-out workshop at The James Beard Foundation in New York for which she received an "outstanding contributor" recognition.

As a culinary consultant, Alamelu has trained chefs at the Kohl's Corporate Innovation Center in Menomonee Falls, Wisconsin, and several other corporate facilities. Now, her recipes are used by the corporate chefs to prepare and serve luncheon meals to employees on a daily basis.

Alamelu is a graduate of the College of Health Sciences at the University of Wisconsin-Milwaukee and resides in Milwaukee, Wisconsin, and Scottsdale, Arizona.

Be sure to follow Alamelu's Facebook page **"Healthful Indian Flavors with Alamelu,"** for blog posts and recipe tips or visit **www.curryonwheels.com.**

Also by Alamelu Vairavan . . .

HEALTHFUL INDIAN FLAVORS WITH ALAMELU

*"I highly recommend **Healthful Indian Flavors with Alamelu** to readers who want to take advantage of the powerful, healing antioxidant qualities of spices and at the same time, indulge in the flavor-rich, wholesome offerings of Indian cuisine."*

—Dr. Bharat Aggarwal, Author of
Healing Spices
Former Professor, University of Texas
MD Anderson Cancer Center

This cookbook contains recipes featured on the first three seasons of Alamelu Vairavan's popular Milwaukee Public Television/PBS cooking show, "Healthful Indian Flavors with Alamelu," along with updated and improved recipes from her previously published cookbooks.

Included are more than 120 flavorful Indian favorites—each with a full color photo—that are sure to please fans old and new. With a focus on vegetables and protein-rich legumes, the recipes include soups, curries, crunchy salads, and a host of vegetarian specialties that are not only low-calorie and low-fat, but packed with nutrients, fiber and flavor. Step-by-step instructions and a helpful guide to spices and ingredients make it easy for readers to create authentic Indian dishes at home.

Also available in e-book format wherever e-books are sold.

ISBN 0-7818-1358-1 · $19.95 paperback

HEALTHY SOUTH INDIAN COOKING
Expanded Edition
Alamelu Vairavan and Dr. Patricia Marquardt

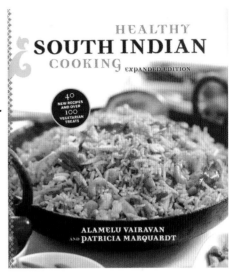

"Coconut-infused curries, brilliant vegetable dishes . . . what could be complex becomes relatively simple in Vairavan's approach . . ."
—Los Angeles Times

"Besides 100 feast-worthy vegetarian recipes, [the authors] explain how the spices that make Indian cuisine so fragrant and flavorful also pack a whallop of nutrients and disease-fighting phytochemicals."
—Wisconsin State Journal

"Dals, chutneys and curries take their place along with fare that might be totally new to many . . . the authors do a remarkably good job of keeping the recipes relatively simple and accessible."
—The Post-Crescent

In the famous Chettinad cooking tradition of southern India, these mostly vegetarian recipes allow home cooks to create dishes such as Potato-filled Dosas with Coconut Chutney; Pearl Onion and Tomato Sambhar; Chickpea and Bell Pepper Poriyal; and Eggplant Masala Curry. *Rasams*, breads, legumes and *payasams* are all featured here, as is the exceptional Chettinad Chicken Kolambu, South India's version of the popular *vindaloo*. Each of these low-fat, low-calorie recipes come with a complete nutritional analysis. Also included are sample menus and innovative suggestions for integrating South Indian dishes into traditional Western meals. A section on the varieties and methods of preparation for *dals* (a lentil dish that is a staple of this cuisine), a multilingual glossary of spices and ingredients, and 16 pages of color photographs make this book a clear and concise introduction to the healthy, delicious cooking of South India.

ISBN: 0-7818-1189-9 · $35.00hc